I DEDICATE THIS BOOK TO ALL MY FRIENDS IN HEAVEN, WHO TAUGHT ME THAT LIFE CAN BE OVER SO QUICKLY AND THAT EVERY DAY IS PRECIOUS. THINKING OF YOU, MISSING YOU, ADORING YOU!

Dear wonderful lady, I'm so honored that you are here! This book is two books in one. The first part is "only for men."

YOUR book starts on page 169 and it's beautifully designed!

But first, listen, if you have a partner, you would love to take on your self-development journey, but he would never ever touch this book with the current cover design: I have a secret plan to share with you.

Download the "cover design for men" from my website www.joyismycompass.com/cover, print it, cut it out and wrap the book with it. With that trick I hope that you get your man to read the book and that he will be all in for creating your dream life together!

If you like this trick, but you don't want him to see this page ;) cut it out. There is nothing printed on the back, for just this reason.

Now it's your turn. I welcome you again on page 169 and I'm super excited to start this journey with you! Let's sit down and drink coffee or tea, it's on me.

Ronja ♡

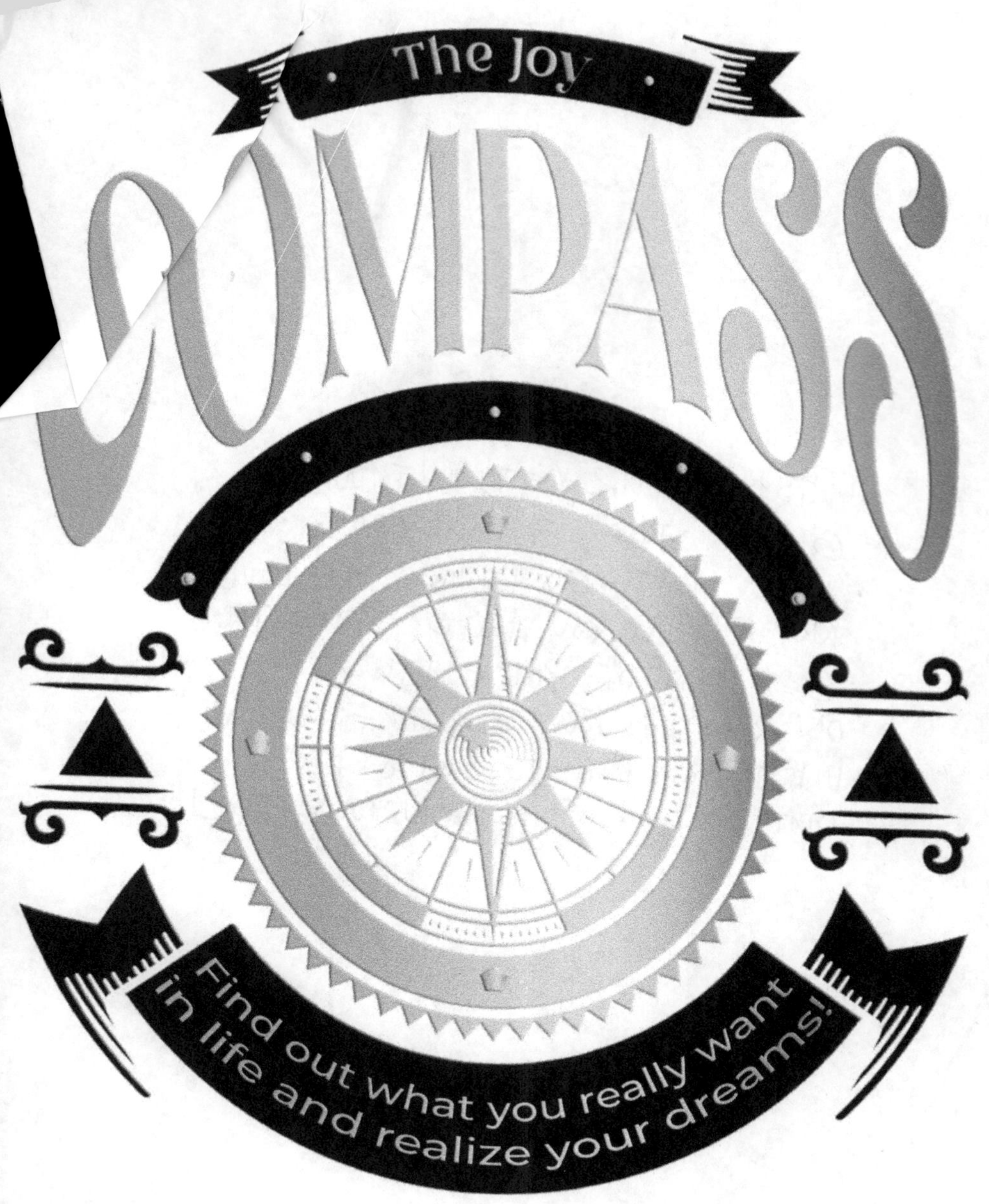

The Joy
COMPASS
Find out what you really want
in life and realize your dreams!
Ronja Sakata

"THIS IS YOUR LIFE WITHOUT A GUARANTEE OF HOW LONG IT WILL LAST. DO THINGS YOU LOVE NOT THINGS YOU HATE! MAKE THE BEST OUT OF YOUR TIME HERE ON EARTH, BUT FIRST FIND OUT WHAT YOU WANT. LET'S FIND OUT WITH A SMILE ON YOUR FACE!"

Hey Man,

I'm honored that you are here! This book is only for guys.
Imagine we're having a beer or two in a pub and we're talking
about the topics of this book together. I am very direct and
don't fuss around. You can talk back to me anytime. I love "in
your face"-language. My goal is to push you into action.

Action to think and find out what <u>you</u> want to change in your
life step by step. I want to talk you into techniques and tools
you might have never tried. You'll find your own superpowers
with them. You need yourself and some time to do that.

You've got this, let's go!

Cheers!

Ronja

MY GIFT
TO YOU!
www.joyismycompass.com/wooho
DOWNLOAD THE
AUDIOBOOK
FOR FREE

CONTENTS

1

"WE CANNOT CURE THE WORLD OF SORROWS,
BUT WE CAN CHOOSE TO LIVE IN JOY"

JOSEPH CAMPELL

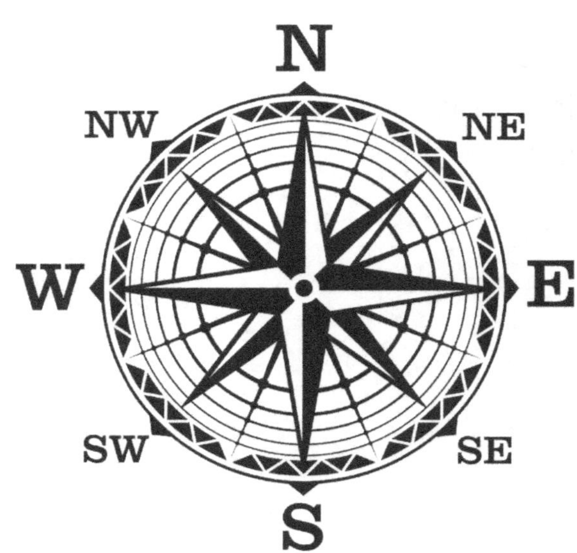
N
NW
NE
W
E
SW
SE
S

CHAPTER ONE

MY OWN STORY

GAME OVER

He was a tough guy with deep thoughts. One you don't get a grip of. A really free spirit. Motorbike tours and outdoor sports were his thing. I was seventeen when I stood at his open grave. He was killed in an avalanche in the Swiss mountains. Four people of a group of ten died. Six families were celebrating life, four families and friends experienced the brutal fact that this life-game is not forever. You have no guarantee for any day or year...any moment could be your last. It's hard to learn that at seventeen years old, but I guess it doesn't depend on age. The first time you are totally aware of this fact... it's a punch in your face.

Eleven years followed with too many funerals of friends my age. A motorbike-accident, another avalanche, a suicide—and then the best friend of my sister died, at the age of twenty-five, because of a sudden heart attack. Oh wow... no dangerous sport involved, no risky ski-tour, no overlooked speed limit. She was at home. Her boyfriend, who was a med-school student, did all he could to bring her back... but she was gone.

THIS was the funeral I decided to no longer live by any compromises. From that day on I decided I would live my life on my own terms.

Today, I no longer do things I don't like. I don't do things to please others. If I do anything or say anything or go anywhere, I do it because I WANT TO! This is simple, isn't it? Maybe you already live by this principle? I was already doing a good job at it back then, too—remember, my wakeup call came at seventeen. But at that moment, I really got into the game of life. I could be dead tomorrow, so TODAY I live life to the fullest. I enjoy my day! I'm as kind as I can be to everybody I meet. I do what I want. I spend time with people I love. I treasure the people I love. I go to places I want to see. I take care of my body. I'm ALL IN.

I really believe that we don't need a wakeup call like an illness, a catastrophe, an accident, a death or a near-death experience to be "all in," though that does help to see the urgency of this topic. You are reading this book, and that's everything you need right now! Well, not everything...YOU have to do the work, you have to figure out what YOU want in your life. You have to decide that this day today is your BEST, and tomorrow will be even better! YOU CHOOSE!

That's so damn powerful. Do you get that? You are my hero because you are curious enough to read this book. You are a really cool guy that you are open enough to give this girl from Switzerland a chance to talk to you.

Have you heard of the book, *The Top Five Regrets of the Dying*? Bronnie Ware is the author, and she collected these top five regrets from uncountable conversations with dying people at her work as a nurse. They are:

1. I wish I'd had the courage to live a life true to myself, not the life others expected of me.
2. I wish I hadn't worked so hard.
3. I wish I'd had the courage to express my feelings.
4. I wish I had stayed in touch with my friends.
5. I wish that I had let myself be happier.

What do you think when you read through these? You can read the book, of course, for deeper inspiration, but let's think about these points for YOUR life right now. Let's do this, okay?

1. I wish I'd had the courage to live a life true to myself
Let's find out what a life true to yourself looks like! The expectations of your parents, your spouse, your neighbors, drop them! They are not helpful. Don't drop the relationships, just the expectations. YOU design a life you are happy with, and I promise you the people in your life can only benefit from this clear decision. You'll be free and feel great—and feeling great is so damn helpful when enjoying the life which is true to yourself!

2. I wish I hadn't worked so hard.
Only you know if you are working "too hard." One day you'll regret that you missed all the family things or the activities with your friends. We'll dig into finding that balance in the book, because hey, we have work to do, right?

3. I wish I'd had the courage to express my feelings.
Is this sentence scaring you already? Maybe you are thinking, "Feelings are reserved for the ladies. I am cool and have my shit together; who would want to express their feelings, anyway? I'm a MAN!" No worries: You are the captain of your life. You decide. Nobody can tell you to do it this or that way, but think about this regret. We'll work on it!

4. I wish I had stayed in touch with my friends.
Taking care of the friends you have—the ones from elementary school and the ones you met recently—is pure gold. Let's step up the "friends" game. Spend time

with them. Talk to them. Support them. You'll get everything back, tenfold.

5. I wish that I had let myself be happier. Happiness is a choice. However, there are some things to tackle before it gets easier and more fun to choose happiness. That my friend, we'll work through in this book. You are in charge of your life. YOU design it, you create it, YOU are one hundred percent responsible for everything in your life. As soon as you own it, own your mood, own your thoughts, and own your actions. You are damn free to be happy any time of the day. Too good to be true? Too sickly sweet? Give me a chance and read this book. You can judge me afterward, ok? My goal is to persuade you to create a life that is better than your wildest dreams... and I can do it! I'm the girl who wants to be your partner in crime!

> My whole life, I enjoyed being around men. While studying at the ETH Zurich (Swiss Federal Institute of Technology) I lived together with four guys in a shared apartment. I loved it. It was so much fun, and communication was so easy. If I'd said to them, "Shut up, asshole," they wouldn't think our friendship was over. They knew I just meant that they should shut up and that I found them to be an asshole in that instant.

You get that, right? Well, you're a guy, I don't have to explain that to you. But that's the reason I decided to write two books: One for the guys and one for the ladies. Just leave this book with the ladies-cover up on the coffee table and your girlfriend, your wife, your daughter will be curious to know what that book is all about. In return, I'll tell her in the girls' book to relax more when it comes to guys, okay? To not expect that you'll text her every minute and that if you don't, that doesn't mean you want to break up with her the next morning. I'll tell her to take care of her own happiness, that you and your actions are not responsible for her mood. I'll tell her that she can buy her own flowers, if she wants flowers.

Are you smiling right now? Or do you disagree, and think, "Hey I MAKE my girl happy and I'll do whatever she wants to keep her happy"?

Well, we might have some things to discuss in this book either way. I don't say, by any means, that only I am right! I just think it would be so much easier on this planet if men and women would relax more and wouldn't overthink everything the other sex is doing-thinking-meaning all the time. It's so much easier to say what you want, say what you think, and set the other person free to act as she or he wants without any expectations. We'll get to that topic later. And hey, if you want to have a look on the other side of the book, you might learn something too!

Have you heard about the wheel of life? In a team-building workshop of your company? In a magazine? It's nothing more than a graph in the shape of a wheel that lines out all the areas of your life on spokes. You can rate yourself where you're at, and where you want to be!

"I want ten out of ten in all areas, baby!"

Okay! Well, you've got some work to do! Ah, you want to get everything without effort? Sorry, my dear friend, that's not gonna happen. But I swear, I have some tools up my sleeves which will help you enormously to get faster and easier to where you want to be…you just have to keep reading.

I think we're getting along very nicely, don't you think? You can swear anytime, by the way, and call me a stupid bitch, if you want to. Tell me I should fuck off if I annoy you, okay? I don't care. I just want you to keep reading and do the work. Think about the questions, and be brutally honest with yourself.

Nobody will ever know that you've read this book and worked through it. I won't tell anybody. But I promise you, people will notice the difference. They'll notice you are not so serious anymore, or not so stressed, or more playful, or in better shape, in a better mood, your posture filled with energy, you don't get angry immediately, or you all of a sudden speak up and say what YOU want! Oh, it will be so much fun to watch your friends' faces acknowledging that you've changed. They won't be able to grasp it, but they will feel the difference—and so will you. You will be bold and present, you will be filled with power and energy, you will be kinder and wiser...

"Um, lady... what was your name again... Ronja? Don't exaggerate, okay? You're a dreamer. I won't change so dramatically!?"

Well, you can if you want to!

"But only with a book? Are you kidding?"

You're right, a book can't do all that—this book only has advice on how to change your life to the party YOU want it to be. Only YOU have the power to actually change. But let's stop fussing around and start, okay? All you have to do is just answer the questions in each chapter really honestly. Write the answers down. Trust me, when you read what you've written a year from now, you won't be able to believe the difference you've made. In a year, you can congratulate yourself again and again for your bravery in starting this journey with me! Let's go, man!

2

> ## "THE BAD NEWS IS TIME FLIES. THE GOOD NEWS IS YOU'RE THE PILOT"
>
> MICHAEL ALTSHULER

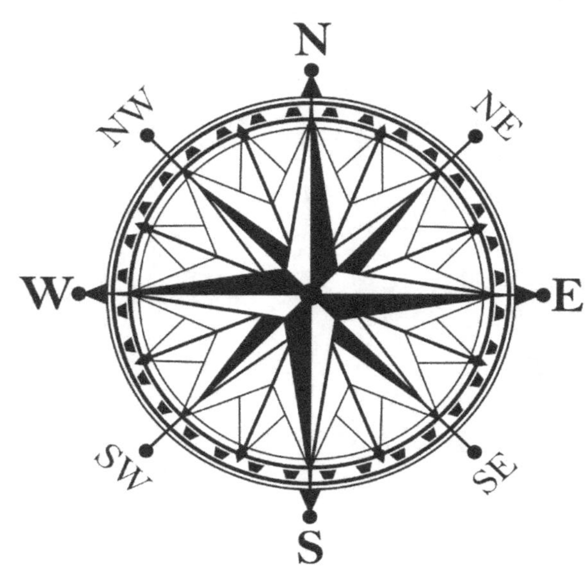

MY BIG FAT VISION

EVERYTHING IS POSSIBLE

What do you want? Did you ever hear that question when you were a little boy, or was everything decided for you? When I ask this question in my personal coaching, lots of people cringe.

"I don't know!" they say. "I have to go to work, right? I have to earn money... so why should it be important what I want?"

I want to switch things around here. First we'll find out what you WANT, and then we'll figure out a way to get it, okay? Remember, life could be over in a second! Why on earth should you waste your time doing things you don't like… or even hate? I mean it. I want to go through every aspect of your life to get super clear on what it is, that YOU want!

Imagine this big fat vision like a lighthouse in your future. It shines its light on your sea of life—be it consisting of rough waves or clear water—and you are on your way to getting there. You are the captain of your ship, so YOU decide. My goal of this book is to help you realize exactly that until you feel it in your bones and say, "Hell YEAH! I'm the captain of my life, and I can be and do and have whatever I want."

If you think I'm a stupid dreamer, no problem. Call me whatever you want, just keep reading!

ONE-HUNDRED-YEAR-OLD YOU

One-hundred-year-old you sitting on the porch, looking back on your life. Ready for a thought-experiment? If you're really brave, you can get the one hundred-year-old meditation on the book-bonus page and surf through your thoughts that way. Try it! You don't have to tell anybody that you meditated! And if you are an old crack in meditating, do it anyway. I'll guide your mind, and you'll have great insights for sure! You can get the meditation for free, here: www.joyismycompass.com/bookbonus

If you think I'm crazy for suggesting that you meditate any day of the next decade, fine. We can do this without closed eyes... you fraidy-cat!

Imagine you are one hundred years old; your body is strong, well trained, and healthy. You are in very good shape, physically and mentally. You are super relaxed and alert at the same time, like a puma. You're sitting on your porch or in your garden or at the beach... where are you? Imagine wherever you feel totally comfortable, because this is YOUR future self sitting there. Are you at the beach? In the mountains? Is the air hot and humid or cool and fresh? Ask yourself: Where am I? Choose your dream destination and the conditions you feel best in... and then close your eyes as your one hundred-year-old self and look back on your life. You feel so damn grateful for everything you've experienced and achieved. You have a grin on your face when you think of all the trouble you went through, knowing how it made you stronger. You feel, deep in your heart, how powerful you've always been on your journey. You are proud of yourself that you took care of yourself, your body, and your mind. Now let your mind wander in your memories.

- **Where have you travelled? Close and far? Did you go to the places you always wanted to?**

- **What did you do for a living? I'm sure you didn't do one damn job you hated, instead you did so many wonderful things and influenced others around you.**

Maybe you invented things or changed jobs and companies for the better.

- With whom did you spend your time? Do you have a partner? Did you have a partner but she or he already passed? Do you have kids? Grandkids? Dogs? Other pets?

Imagine your friendships, your gang, your partners in crime. Imagine the ladies and gentlemen you adored and hopefully still adore. Let your mind wander and explore these precious memories.

- How did you live, and where do you live now?

Just think of the rich and fulfilled lifetime you had, and realize that, hey, it's not over yet! You have many possibilities, to go on a bike tour, to help your granddaughter found her business. You are so fit and healthy. You feel ready for many more years to come on YOUR terms, with all the people in your life you love, with all the adventures you still have on your bucket list— even though you did a damn great job to do loads of things you wanted to experience up until now.

Everybody around you calls you "the lucky guy," but you know it wasn't luck—it was YOUR work and determination. You created this life because you wanted it. It feels so good. You have a big smile on your face and feel deeply grateful for everything which was possible. If you believe in God or the Universe or some bigger force, you say thank you to whom it may concern.

Is that too cheesy for you? Or did you feel it? Can you imagine that this is even a possibility? One of my friends yelled at me when I told her about this exercise. "One hundred years? Are you kidding me? At eighty years I'm done and OUT!"

Okay... I never thought about it this way. I want to stay in the game as long as possible. I know that today or tomorrow my life could be over, but my plans and my vision, they go beyond one hundred years for sure. I like it here. I like this world. I like everybody I meet. I like YOU! I love spending time with you in this book. Maybe we'll meet in person someday somewhere. Everything is possible. Adidas said it in negative words, but I loved their slogan: Impossible is nothing! Do you believe me? Do you hear me? Everything is possible. But first you have to know what you want.

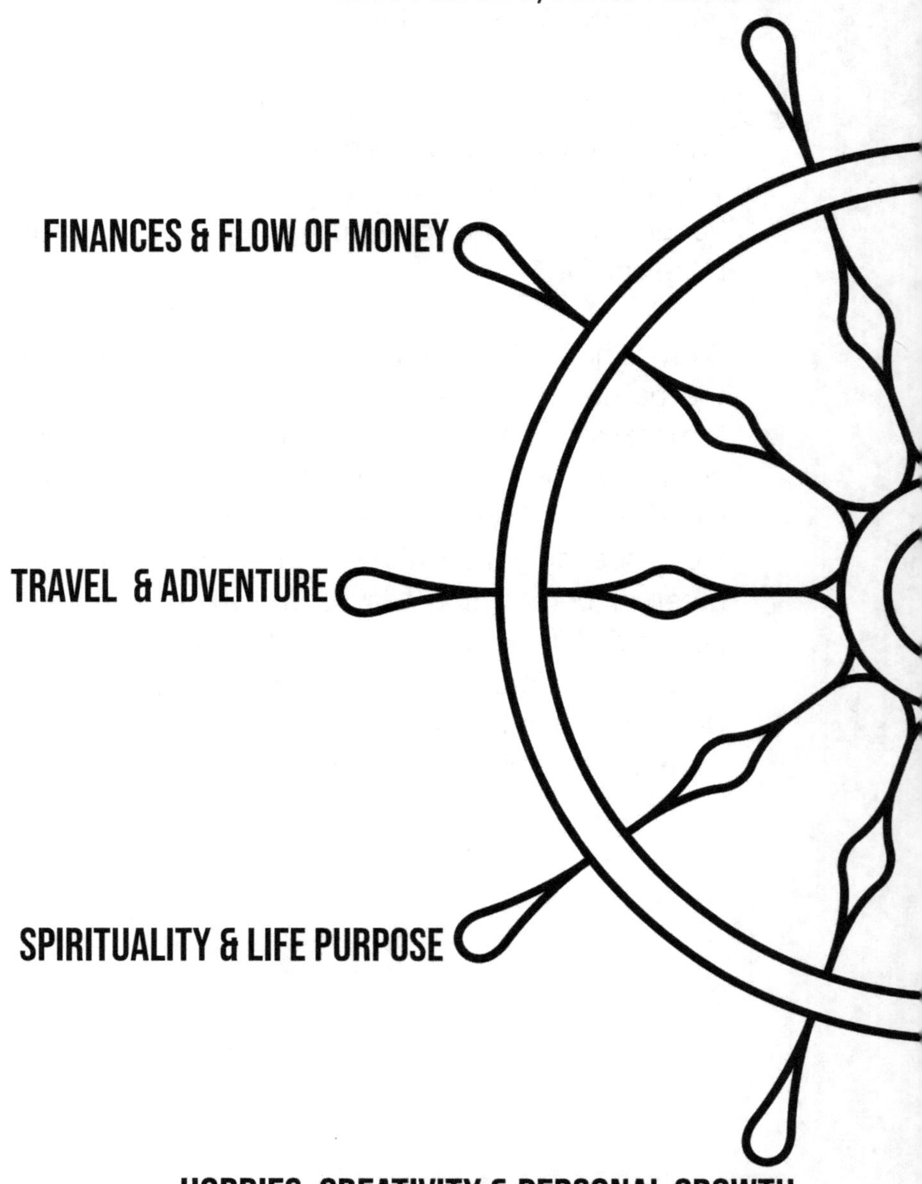

ZEST FOR LIFE, FUN & FREE TIME
FINANCES & FLOW OF MONEY
TRAVEL & ADVENTURE
SPIRITUALITY & LIFE PURPOSE
HOBBIES, CREATIVITY & PERSONAL GROWTH

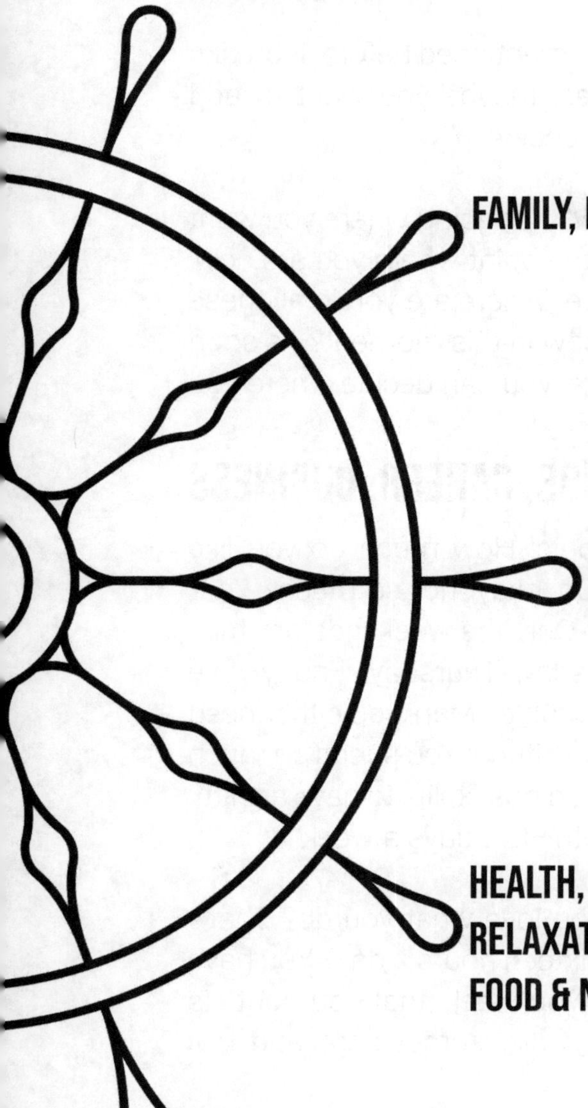

LOVE LIFE & ROMANCE
FAMILY, FRIENDS & RELATIONSHIP
LIVING SPACE,
PHYSICAL ENVIRONMENT
HEALTH, PHYSICAL FITNESS,
RELAXATION & WELLNESS
FOOD & NURTURE
DAILY JOB, CAREER & BUSINESS

WHEEL OF LIFE

Let's go to this wheel of life I mentioned before. It breaks your life into ten categories. Maybe you want to add another spoke or two? You decide.

First step: Where am I NOW? For going where you want to go, the GPS first needs the point where you are now. Let's be brutally honest here. Where are you in all these different categories, right now in this moment? As soon as you reveal where you are, you can decide where you want to go.

DAILY JOB, CAREER, BUSINESS

Let's start with an easy topic! How much do you like what you do for a living? Oh, okay…not so much? Your work sucks? No fun at all? Only the weekends are fun? Monday, Tuesday, Wednesday, Thursday, Friday—five days of the week are just horrible? Man, you either need a different job or a different attitude! You spend so much time at work that it's just not a possibility to have a shitty job or a shitty mood—or both—five days a week!

Ah—your job is brilliant? You love what you do? That's good news! But you work sixteen hours a day? You have no private life at all? You feel that burnout is approaching in big steps from somewhere and will reach you soon?

Or is your job wonderful? Do you jump out of bed in the morning and love what you do?

If the last sentence makes you cringe and you think, "Shut up, you dreamer-bitch," you have some changes to make! Or, better said, you have a huge potential to improve this area of your life. I swear, if you are in a job or career situation where you hate every day (or most of your day), you'll get sick, have one of these trendy burnouts, or—have you heard about bore-outs? That's when you are overwhelmed with the boring job you're doing day in and day out! Anyway, something will occur to get you on YOUR road again.

As you are reading this, I hope to shake you hard enough so you wake up and turn this ride around, so you can enjoy what you're doing, and so you are satisfied in the evening with what you've accomplished. Yes, this IS POSSIBLE! Yes, with ANY kind of education. Yes, you'll make enough money with your dream job—no, actually, you'll make more money than ever by doing what you love and what you're good at!

"But my dad expects me to be a lawyer... but my grandfather told me to become a craftsman... I don't want to disappoint anyone."

Really? But you want to punish yourself every day with a job you hate?

A job is a huge mix of expectations, from your family, your boss, your coworkers, and yourself. The relationships with yourself, your team, your family, and your whole company makes it better or even worse.

The questions you have to ask yourself are:

- Do I like my job?
- What do I like about my job?
- What do I dislike?
- What would I love to do for a living if I could choose freely and money would not be an issue?
- What am I really good at doing? Think about everything you're good at!
- What do I like doing? Think of anything you enjoy doing!
- Do I like to work with people? If yes, how? If no, what would be your preferred work setting?

Did you feel uncomfortable reading these questions? Or did you tell me to fuck off with this? Or you're not interested in thinking about the answers at all? Well…I don't care, as long as you keep reading. You can decide how you want to work, and you DESERVE a job you like— or better, love!

Maybe this is the time to change things?

"But hey, I can't change my work! I need this work to pay my bills!"

I don't mean to tell you, "Quit your job today with no Plan A in your pocket." (Plan B is running at the moment, don't you agree?) I only ask you to think about these questions NOW, and write down your thoughts!

"I won't write anything… stupid lady!"
Oh nice, you didn't say "bitch" this time. But I say, shut up and think AND WRITE!

Again: What do I like about my job right now? What do I enjoy? What's working out? What do I want to have in any job I'm doing?

What do I dislike about my job right now? What's the problem? What would I change TODAY if I could? What do I need to change so I can say: I get up in the morning, and I look forward to going to work?

What could be MY part in this changing game? Could I show up with more presence? What would that look like? How do I want to show up, anyway?

What's my work attitude? How could I do my job with more excellence? How would I be different, if I would give my current job my everything?

"Oh come on! I just work for money. I don't care how I 'show up' and blah blah blah…"

I like how you get angry! You seem to care, anyway.

Man, try to imagine your work to be a cool place to go, where you're having a blast, doing what you like, with awesome guys and ladies. Imagine a life where, in the evening, you're really happy with your day!

Does this still sound very stupid?

If you are not even willing to consider an improvement, that's your choice! Anything is your choice. You design your wheel of life on every spoke. If you think that sucks, you could flip it and ponder over the possibility that you really have the power to create anything you want in your life. Remember, it could be over today, or tomorrow, or even in ten minutes...

I like to think of life as a big playground where I can choose everything—my mood, my attitude, my actions, my way of interacting with the creatures around me, and even how I interact with things. If this is the case, my job, which takes up so many hours a day, better be a good one!

I always liked seeing my completed day's work in the evening. The most satisfying job I ever had was filling Japanese salad dressing bottles. One at a time. I got really quick at this very robotic work. It was very monotonous and very boring, but we had lots of good conversations while hundreds, then thousands of bottles piled up neatly packed in boxes. The best thing was that it was MY salad dressing company I did this work for. Seeing the work as a real "thing" in the tiny factory hall was so pleasing to me. During that time, I started listening to audiobooks. Getting inspiration and learning interesting concepts while doing the things you could do with your eyes closed is so cool! It's also the best thing to do on your commute. Traffic jam, long rides? No problem—I'm replenishing myself over my ears. There are podcasts for free on every topic! Try it!

"But I'm not even allowed to listen to music at work!"

You could ask if you could change that, or discuss when it would be okay to have your earphones plugged in. First you could try this while you do private things in and around the house.

One guy I was listening to while doing the salad dressing job was Jens Corssen. I had the honor to attend a whole day-long event where he spoke to us about all his concepts. His audiobook, *The Way of the Self-Developer: Your Path to Personal & Professional Success*, is more than brilliant, and all the stories he told us at the event were on repeat in my ears, so I'll never forget them! One story was about apprentices in a hotel he trained in mindset. They decided that from then on they'll think it's cool to carry suitcases of wealthy guests from the car to the front desk. That they'll go all in to do this job, smiling at the guests, and doing the job with excellence. They became the best porters of all time, but nothing would have changed without a vision of the dream job in their minds. Being clear about what you want WHILE doing your current job with excellence...THAT'S the big secret for success, and having your personal dream job sooner or later.

Yes, back to you, my friend! Do you know what your dream job is? Ask yourself:

What would I adore to do for a living if I could choose freely and money would not be an issue?

Oh, come on, stay with me for this! I mean it! Think about this. Think about any activity you love that you would love to earn money with! We are living in the internet times. We have the best opportunities to earn money with anything we can think of! The world waits at your doorstep... or in front of billions of computers. If you're not thinking of a career online, offline jobs are brilliantly supported by the internet for connecting, producing, printing, reporting...the possibilities are endless.

- **Think about everything you're good at! Write it down...**

- **Think of anything you enjoy doing... you might create your new job right here and now!**

- **Do you like to work with people? If yes how? If no, what would be your preferred work setting?**

- Would you like to create something to sell? Would you rather like to teach, support, connect…?

- Write about your dream job and note ideas, activities, and things you'd love to do. Do this brainstorming, then pin the ideas above your kitchen table.

- WHAT do you want to do for work?

Then dream about it. Imagine working at your new dream job before you fall asleep at night.

"Ronja, don't tell me to do things like this. That's so lame… "

Try it, my friend. Try it and stop thinking that you are not the kind of person who does exercises like this. Just do it. And note the difference! Okay? You don't have to tell anybody about the changes you are making in your head. You can keep all this as a secret. Your buddies, they'll never know… but hey, what if you do tell them? THAT would be so cool, because then you would all know that you are worth living your best life, not a boring-lame-stressful one.

But first, it's about YOU! I don't care who you'll talk about all this with, or if you don't tell anybody. YOU will have the benefits of this thought- and action-work.

So, you will imagine yourself doing the coolest, most awesome job ever, earning a ton of money while having fun before you fall asleep at night. During the day, DON'T compare your current job with your dream job. Don't complain. Instead, do your work with a new commitment, new power, and new energy.

Try to not complain about anything for a week, and note the difference in you! Try to go all in at work for a week. You'll feel totally different the next Monday morning. Nothing changed besides what you're thinking. I love that. It's free, it's working, it's a decision you can make in one second.

I bet your boss will recognize the difference. Maybe other people at work call you out. Maybe your co-workers get pissed off, that you are Happy Harry all of a sudden... They'll overcome it for sure. Step by step, you'll influence them without saying a word!

You never know if, by changing your attitude, your current job will change into your dream job. Or maybe you will get an offer from your company to do another job. Whatever will happen, I promise you that your chances for promotion or other good things are at least a million percent up, now that you've changed your work attitude. Do you agree? Can you see my point? Are we on the same page?

I love you for doing this with me! I'm in awe that you are reading this book, I really am! Most men in my life don't read books, so I'm extra proud of you for being in the game.

You did a great job thinking and dreaming about how you want to earn your money in the future (sometime…eventually…if possible! Not so much momentum in these statements, huh?). So, what do you do to make these dreams come true? If you do something every day, you'll reach your goal for sure. Go you! In the job-career-department, wherever you work, however you feel right now, you've got this! Your dream job is out there, so go and get it, or go and create it!

FAMILY / RELATIONSHIPS AND LOVE LIFE / ROMANCE

You won't need any help to figure out the travel spoke, but I want to work through the family/relationships and love life/romance topic with you together! Okay? Ready?

From one to ten, where are you on these two spokes? Generally, in the big picture?

Let's say you have a brilliant lady in your life who is super confident and doing her own thing. Spending time with her is fun and easy. You can make fun of each other and have deep conversations. You spend lots of quality time together, AND you do things alone or with your own peers because that way you have something to tell each other when you come home from a trip with your buddies. You both have big goals in life and help each other achieve them.

Maybe you have kids together and you love them. They trust you, you trust them, and together you are THE family gang, which supports each other no matter what. Your home is filled with laughter and fun. You all communicate openly and with great respect for each other. It's just so damn good to be the dad of this clan!

Let's say you have a great relationship with your parents, and you admire them for their legacy. Your siblings are your cheerleaders, and you all take care of each other.

...Are you still reading? Did you nod and smile and say, "YEP, that's my reality!" ...or did you hate me for this paragraph? How IS your reality?

Are you single and desperately looking for "your other half"? Are you single and very happy that you don't have anybody to care for? Do you have a relationship, but it's a constant disaster?

I know, I mention all the stereotypes and extremes. Only YOU know what is going on in your relationship-department. Only YOU can be brutally honest with yourself, as in the job-discussion ask yourself: How am I doing here? How is it going? And WHAT do I want?

What did you think, when you read the "ideal" family situation above? Did you say, "Ugh, I can't stand this Hollywood-trash!" Or did you think, "Oh yeah, that's the dream, but it's not possible for me"?

While discussing your job situation, I could say: "GO and find a job you like and love! Go and do your current job really well, while you go step by step toward your dream job or business!"

Relationships are much more complex. Much more diverse. You can be a lone wolf and LOVE it, or you can be in the same situation and be very lonely and desperate. Wherever you are on your journey through life and however your relationships and love life look, ask yourself:

WHAT do I want?!

Write that down. Take out your journal (you can hide it from whomever is not allowed to read it...but hey, whoever would find it should be proud of you for doing this work for YOU and the important people in your life. I hope that you have relationships where a personal journal is respected, and no one makes fun of it!) and write down HOW you want to shape this spoke of your wheel of life.

I can ask you similar questions like in your work-situation:

- What do I like about my love life right now? What is going well in my relationships? What am I grateful for? What makes me happy? What's working?

Focus first on what's going well. Write down even the smallest thing you're grateful for. That's something I want to train you to do throughout this book anyway: Focus on the positive things, even though you're aware of what is shitty and miserable. It's better to see the good things first, instead of focusing on everything that's going wrong.

If you haven't written down a word by now, can you please move your ass and go and get a notebook? I mean it! Writing things down is like free therapy.

"THERAPY? I don't need therapy!"
Okay, okay, okay... forget I said that!

I believe that every single person on this planet can profit from talking (or writing) about the things going on in their lives AND about what they want. That way, you can bring your thoughts in order and see things clearer than before.

So, I ask you again: What do you like about your love life right now? What is going well in your relationships? What are you grateful for? What makes you happy? What's working? WRITE your answers down!

- What do you hate about what's going on in your relationships? In your love life? What do you want to change? What can you change?

The good news is: You can only change yourself and nobody else.

The bad news is: You can only change yourself and nobody else.

Ha, ha... not funny? It's just a fact, and I think it's a good one!

Taking full responsibility for yourself is much easier than taking responsibility for everyone around you. If you are fully aware of this fact, you can focus only on YOU! How do I speak with the people around me? How do I treat the people around me? By "people" I mean your spouse, your girlfriend, your buddies, your kids, your friends, your neighbors, and the random folks you meet at the supermarket and in the park.

- How do I want to BE in my relationships? How do I want to play the game of life within my family and in my love life? What do I think of others? How do I judge others? How do I talk to myself in my thoughts? How do I judge myself?

Lots of things to think about, right?
What do you want?

Write YOUR ideal situation down, even though you might think that this will never happen. This only happens to the other guys, not you, right? Nope! Impossible is nothing—or, in positive words: Everything is possible. YOU can change YOU, and that's enough to change everything around you. Cool?

Your notebook should be full of notes by now... don't read any further before you do your journaling!

I taught food technologists at a professional school for twelve years. In Switzerland, we have a system of learning a profession after nine years of school. It's a combination of working and going to school. After three years, you have a practical and a theoretical test, and if you pass, you're a professional painter or baker or carpenter—or in my case, food technologist. My students were working in chocolate factories and beer breweries, or making cookies, pasta, potato chips, and any other processed food you can imagine. I had a great time with these students, who were between the ages of fifteen and eighteen. I had two rules in my classroom: You are nice to me; I am nice to you. For everything else, I asked them to please use common sense. Maybe I was a little too easy-going, but hey, what do you remember from your schooldays? It's not what you had to learn in the classes, right? It's the fun in between classes, the teachers you loved, the friends you made. I loved all my students (in a total of 800 within these twelve years there were maybe five complete idiots... that's an okay rate!), and we had a great relationship. Relationships are the key to learning and growing, right? And if they didn't do the homework, I wasn't upset at all... they had to do it for THEMSELVES. If they didn't do it, that wasn't my problem. I was good at letting go and having no expectations. That's how I had them do more in my classes than in all the other subjects. They felt responsible for their own learning. (Bragging me...but wait, I have a point!)

So, what about YOU? Are you willing to do your homework for YOURSELF? Don't do this for me! I won't check, if you did it or not, I don't care! Actually, I DO care, but I have to hand the responsibility over to you, because it's your life.

I want to have the same respectful and fun relationship with you as I had with my students. The big difference is that I don't have to test you. You don't have to memorize the structure and process of a pasta-dryer in great detail and explain it in a test. I don't know more than you. You are the expert of your life. But when it comes to changing it, you need to do the work! You need to do the homework for yourself. Got it?

What do I want to change in my relationship-game? Can I be more present? Can I listen better? Can I just give my love a big bear hug instead of arguing over the same shit as always? Can I say clearly what I need and want, in order to have the relationship I wish for? Do I know what I want? How would my relationships change if I step up my game and bring JOY into it?

Choose to answer the questions you like best!

Take some time off for thinking and writing. You don't have time? Switch off your T.V. or put down the phone. I'm sure that you'll find time! And hey, it's so worth it! I can't wait to hear from you, to hear how you're ROCKING it and how happy you are that you did this journaling-shit because it was the beginning of changing YOU. With changing yourself, your surroundings slowly change, too.

We'll talk a lot about your living space and physical environment in the next chapter. We'll tackle health, wellness, physical fitness and food in the self-care part of the book. For the remaining topics, you just have to be very honest with yourself.

If you want, you can print out the wheel of life or just write directly in the book. In every topic, ask yourself: What's the current state of my life in this area? How is it going? Am I happy with the status quo? What rate would you give yourself from one to ten? And—super important—WHY? Give me reasons why you gave yourself this rating! These insights are super valuable for yourself. WHY do I think or feel that way?

Next, as we did on the previous spokes, ask: What do I really, really want? What's my dream—the dream I maybe never said out loud because I learned as a kid not to talk about my dreams…

What do you want to do in your free time for your personal fun? How do you bring your zest of life to a new level? Where do you want to travel? What kind of adventure do you want to experience before you die? What do you want to learn? Skydiving? Rock climbing? Cooking? Are you creative, but don't give yourself time for it? Maybe you like woodcarving? Gardening? Painting? Creating music? What is your life purpose? What is the thing you want to leave behind, when you're gone? What shall be your legacy? And hey, how much money do you want to make? More than you make now? Millions? Billions? Everything is possible! Don't believe me? Let's proceed!

I have two very cool and easy exercises ready so you can get even clearer on what you want.

"No, no more questions please!"
Okay, got it. No more questions. Maybe.

BE - DO - HAVE

This exercise is so much fun and it's super easy.
It means that you think about what you want to be, what you want to do, and what you want to have in your life.

Write a list, like a wishlist to Santa:

- **I want to be happy and successful.**
- **I want to be strong.**
- **I want to be fit and healthy.**
- **I want to be a New York Times bestselling author.**
- **I want to be a good husband.**
- **I want to be the best boyfriend ever.**

Just check in with what you want to BE, and write it ALL down. (Yes in your journal, Mister! If someone finds it, she or he will be impressed. Having big dreams is inspiring!)

NEXT: What do you want to DO in your life?
Not, "I want to do awesome things." Be more specific:
I want to exercise every day.
I want to write a book.
I want to win a certain sport event.
I want to run a marathon or an ultra-marathon.
I want to build a "she shed" in my garden for my lady.
What do you want to do in your life, from morning to evening?

What do you want to do as your hobbies, in your job, in your family? Write whatever comes to your mind: What do I want to DO?

The last one, HAVE, can either be materialistic or an achievement like:
I want to have a great relationship with my parents/kids/partner.

I want to have a BMW so and so.
I know nothing about cars, sorry! I like the colorful ones better... if it's not a camping van, I'm just happy to have a ride from A to B... oh and if your car can heat my ass in winter, I'll be impressed too! ...but YOU know what kind of car you would like to have, so write it down!

I want to have a big house.
Describe it in great detail, because you don't want to just have any big house, you want to have the big house YOU like.

Please check in with your HAVE-list and write only things down which make YOU happy. If you want to impress your neighbors and keep up with the Joneses, it will not make you happy in the long run. Write down what YOU desire and want and will have in your life!

I want to have ....

Everything is possible, just write it down!

Do you know what the difference is between a millionaire and a billionaire? The billionaire writes down his goals twice a day.

I heard that quote from Denise Duffield-Thomas, an Australian, self-made millionaire who is a big inspiration to thousands of women (and men). If you want to influence your lady to be more in-tune with your million-dollar dreams, you might buy her the book *Get Rich, Lucky Bitch* as a gift. She'll love it, and if you are up to another read, you'll get inspired too, for sure!

Writing down your goals is a game changer, whether you want to be a millionaire or just have a better life for you and your family. By writing down what you want to be-do-have, you have your dreams and goals in the front of your mind. You are constantly thinking about them in a good way. Your focus is sharpened, and you'll suddenly be aware of opportunities, see chances, and stumble over signs you didn't recognize before.

What's important is that you write down your BE-DO-HAVE while you're in a good mood. It should be fun and feel great, like, "Hell YEAH, THIS is my future!" It should feel like it's a done deal, that you'll definitely get everything on your list!

I want you to write a be-do-have for right now. What do you wish for NOW? Remember, you can decide to change in an instant. So, if you write down, "I want to have a great relationship with my parents," you are now aware of this goal. Maybe you will call them today, or go and say hi. Maybe you always fight, and it's always a mess? This time you could just listen and give your Mama a big hug. YOU know what you can change and how you can behave differently to change things, just because you've decided to do so. Don't rush. If you have old family patterns running for decades, you might need some time, but only your decision to have a great relationship with your parents (or any person who is important to you) can change things for the better in BIG ways. Try it!

Some things need time, so I want you to write another be-do-have list for "in five years" and another one for "in ten years." You'll see how your goals might get bigger, because you believe that you can make it happen. Some things never change, like the "good relationships", "I want to be happy", or "I want to be successful" goals. You can achieve these things right now by changing your attitude and how you show up at work and with the important people around you.

Always write down the date of the day you wrote the list. It's so cool when you read through old lists and you can say: "CHECK, CHECK, CHECK!" You will be amazed by what you've accomplished! It's really wild, what's possible as soon as you are open to thinking about what you want and then going for it!

Your work:

- Write down a Be-Do-Have for right now or this year.
- Write down a Be-Do-Have for in five years (note the according year. If you write this list in 2021, write "Be-Do-Have for 2026.").
- Write down a Be-Do-Have for in ten years (2030 2031...).

Remember the millionaire and billionaire quote? You decide how often you play around with this exercise. Daily? Weekly? Monthly? I suggest you do it as much as possible, but it should be FUN—not an obligation you don't like to do.

As I told you, it should feel great! Playful! Fun! Feel the goals, feel the things you'll have, see the house and the car. Yeah, maybe this sounds corny, but just do it! You'll see the evidence that this journaling-exercise is GOLD really soon, I swear!

MY IDEAL DAY

Did you do the Be-Do-Have? No? Go and do it, you fool! If you don't put in the effort, nothing will change! It's like pushups. Thinking of pushups won't make you stronger. You have to actually do them. Got it?

If you didn't do the be-do-have you won't do this one either.

Oh, you did the exercise? You really dug deep into your wishes? NICE! Then you'll like this next one...

YOUR IDEAL DAY

What's your ideal day? If you have your be-do-have list in your mind, this is an easy thing to write out. Why do double the work? Because it's a different approach, and we have to convince your subconscious mind that all your dreams are possible. You have to change your mindset to the "achiever and winner" mindset. You have to get rid of your complaining, moaning, bitching around, gossiping, and making fun of others. Instead, put all this energy into what you want to achieve and become. (You don't HAVE TO. You can stay exactly as you are...but if you DECIDE to change, all the power is yours!)

The ideal day exercise goes like this:
Imagine waking up, eyes still closed. Where are you?

"In bed stupid lady!"
No, I mean where are you sleeping? In a hammock in a Costa Rican bungalow? In a king size bed in your mansion?

Really imagine this situation and play around with the gazillions of possibilities. What are you wearing? Are you naked? Boxer shorts? Shiny millionaire-silk-pajamas?

I just had to laugh out loud imagining you in your silk pajamas... but hey, maybe that's what you want!

Is there somebody next to you? Do you have a baby leg in your face, because your child is lying next to you? What would be the perfect, ideal waking-up situation? What do you hear? Waves? Is the window open? Do you feel the breeze?

Open your eyes and look around. Again, where are you? What does this room or place look like? Is it your home? Is it your hotel, during your vacation?

I did this exercise with university students in Switzerland. I gave them only fifteen minutes to write, because I was unsure if they would like it or hate it. After fifteen minutes I stopped them, and one guy yelled, "Hey, don't interrupt me! I didn't even get out of bed yet!" That was a nice confirmation that this journaling prompt can be so much fun.

Go all in! Write down all the details: What time do you get up? Did you have an alarm set? What does the flooring look like? Fluffy carpet? Parquet?

Are you wearing house shoes? Are you barefoot? Design your whole day that way. What's next? What do you want to do next in your ideal perfect day? What do you eat for breakfast? Did somebody prepare it for you?

In my ideal day, I have so many very nice staff! I only do the tasks I love to do, like cooking, but the cleaning up, that's not my job. My staff has super-high salaries, and we treat them like kings and queens. They do their job just perfectly. They love to work at our house. It's a total win-win situation. That's how I want to rule my future. How do you want to have yours?

- **What do you do next? A workout? Paragliding? Wakeboarding? Dog training? Bring your kids to their awesome school? Go to your dream workplace? What do you do for a living? Where is your money coming from? Real estate?**

At a conference of Brendon Burchard (check him out, he is one of my heroes who influenced me highly) I met Mike, a very nice guy. I asked him: What do you do for work? "Oh, I have a real estate business. But the business works best if I'm not around. My staff does a great job, so I stay out of their way. I travel all year long. In summer I'm in Europe and in winter I'm in South Asia or South America." I was so impressed... and inspired! I really don't want to travel all year round. I love to live in one place and travel sometimes, but I work toward my company being a real fun machine to run, with little time needed from my side. I want to only do what I love: Write, speak, coach, put out inspirational content and be creative with videos, paintings, drawings.

So that's my personal dream…WHAT is YOURS?

How is your ideal day proceeding? What do you do next? Spend the afternoon with your lady in a spa?

"No I hate spas!"
Oh okay, so you don't go there, of course!

Choose what you LOVE, what makes you HAPPY, what makes you smile and be in awe of your life. The life you created!

- **What do you do next?**
- **What do you eat?**
- **What do you do for your body?**
- **What do you do for fun?**

What's next? What's next? Write yourself through your entire day until you go to bed again—or hop into your hammock, or your campervan. Include a recap, laying in your bed thinking through your day, being grateful for all the things you were able to be-do-have. Say thank you to whomever you believe in, or just say thank you to yourself, for being awesome! For giving your best! For enjoying your blessings.

DONE!

What do you think about this exercise?

"Stupid shit! Why bother? Never going to happen anyway, so just shut up!"

Really? You've read so far and still hang in the mememe-trap?! Get over yourself, mister! Get into gear and try something new. I know, you might find journaling super wimpy, or exhausting, or just stupid. I DON'T CARE! Just get over it and DO IT.

If you did the exercise and loved it, I won't call you out of course... but I have to deal with the students in the back of the room too. The tough guys. The ones who never smile, because that's already a sign of weakness. The ones who are too cool for anything which might be too womanly. Hey, if you are one of those men, I think you are AWESOME! I like your "no bullshit" attitude. In my classroom, these teenagers in the back with the oh so cool faces...I loved them, and my goal was to crack their hearts open...not today, but someday, just by being nice and staying cool if they said rude things. My happiness does not connect to your behavior. You can do what the fuck you want to do in your life. But hey, you're holding this book in your hand and you're still reading...so maybe this is YOUR time to think about your life in a different way? I think so! And I'm really freaking proud of you, for still being here with me. The Swiss girl, teaching you all these silly things. I will tell you again and again: Just do it, and you'll be amazed—not by me, by YOU and your thoughts and how quickly you'll change. Not for being a "good boy", not for impressing your parents or neighbors or anybody else you might have had to impress in your childhood. Nope! Just for YOU! You being proud of you and your life is the greatest gift you can give yourself. But first, you have to know what you WANT! And by doing all the things in this (very long) chapter, you'll find out what you want. It will become super clear.

You can drop dead today, tomorrow, or when you're one hundred years old...you'll find out when it's too late. So, let's get into the game of LIVING our best lives. Let's create a life you are proud of. Okay?

Remember the five biggest regrets of the dying?

1. I wish I'd had the courage to live a life true to myself, not the life others expected of me.
2. I wish I hadn't worked so hard.
3. I wish I'd had the courage to express my feelings.
4. I wish I had stayed in touch with my friends.
5. I wish that I had let myself be happier.

I think you are super aware of the fact that you are the captain of your ship. Your journey will be a good one on your terms, with the work you WANT to do, with awesome relationships, with loads of things that make you happy and bring you joy.

To achieve all the good things, we have to throw out the things that don't serve us anymore. Ready for some decluttering?

Is that another topic you think is a female thing? Let's check out the next chapter. You are open now to all the freaky things I'll tell you, right? You are in this with me together, right? You will benefit from all these spooky "woo-woo" things, right?

Yep! For sure. Just read and DO THE WORK!

3

"FIND JOY IN EVERYTHING YOU CHOOSE TO DO.
EVERY JOB, RELATIONSHIP, HOME… IT'S YOUR
RESPONSIBILITY TO LOVE IT, OR CHANGE IT"

CHUCK PALAHNIUK

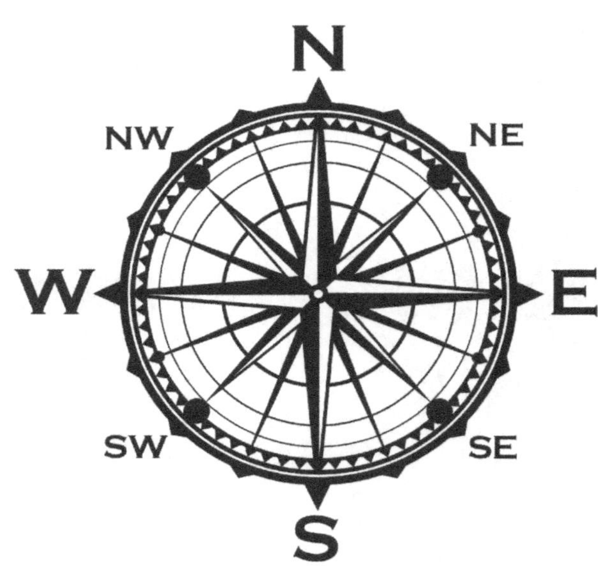

N
NW
NE
W
E
SW
SE
S

CHAPTER THREE

DECLUTTERING OUTSIDE

DON'T LIKE IT? DUMP IT!

When you come home, before you even enter your place...what are you thinking? As you push the door open, what goes through your mind? Nothing? Or do you think, "Dude, this mess is just gross? Who even wants to live here?"

Is it completely the opposite?
"YEAH man, a king lives here. I just love my place!"

Again, I don't know anything about your living space! But you do!

I'm sure you've heard about people who wanted to sell

their house and, to find a buyer, they do a big declutter-session. They paint the fence in a fresh color. The old dead plants in front of the house get replaced by new ones, and so on. The goal: The pictures of the house for the sales page shall look gorgeous. But then, after all the work is done, they realize how stupid they were for living all these years in a place with dead plants in front of the house and a huge mess inside. Maybe they don't even want to move anymore!

You (and your family) deserve a place to live that makes you happy and proud. Who decides on deserving and having this shit? YOU do! You can decide to go all-in and make yourself comfortable at home. You can create a space you are totally proud of.

If you hate having visitors at your place, it's probably because you think it's not elegant enough, not cool enough, not clean enough, and not styled enough. We have these kinds of thoughts when we compare ourselves to friends or people who have fancy houses or living spaces. Forget about the others. Concentrate on YOU!

You can live in a garage, in a tiny house, in a camper van, or in a mansion. You are responsible for doing it YOUR way!

"Yeah, Miss Sakata...I'm responsible for everything. I know, but it sucks to hear that all the time from you."

Hey, imagine it would be the other way around? Imagine if others were responsible for you and your happiness, if others decided how you should live, with whom, where, and how your place is decorated. THAT would be very disturbing, right?

So, OWN this responsibility. It's an honor to take care of yourself and your place and your loved ones.

Don't get me wrong: I'm not a tidy person. As a kid, my mother gave up on me. By the time I was a teenager, she had one rule left for my room: "Keep the door closed!"

Remember the apartment I shared with four guys? It was really dirty, but I really enjoyed this state. Whoever decided something needed cleaning would clean it. It was rarely me, I tell you. The only place I really love to have a clean working space is the kitchen. So, I mostly took care of the kitchen. When Ken, my husband, came to Switzerland from Japan, he moved into my room. One more guy! He had lots of white tennis socks back then. In Switzerland, we have stupid silly "stereotypes" for different states. One state, in particular, is "famous" for people that wear white socks, and everyone makes fun of them. I told Ken that he's risking it if he wears white socks in Zurich. He couldn't care less—BUT, after a week in our apartment, he stated: "I now know why you guys wear black socks! In this place, your socks turn black within an hour anyway."

Yep, it was that bad! But we had a great time together, anyway. When Ken and I moved to our own apartment a year later, it was a really new experience to know that any mess was either my fault or his. No one else to blame.

I'm still messy, and I have to put in a lot of effort to keep my space tidy. Ken is perfect compared to me, and it's annoying! Our daughter has the same chaotic character as me, so he's outnumbered (and whines a lot that he is such a poor guy with us messy ladies). When I have guests, I always clean up. It annoys me that I do this for friends or guests, but not for myself. Do you know that feeling? It's the same when I keep promises I made to everyone else, but not the ones I made to myself. Grrrrr... but again: Only I can change that one.

So, how about making a promise to yourself to live in a place that you admire, are proud of, and where you feel totally in your power? Sound good? Sounds too girly? Just stay with me, and take away what speaks to you, okay? My reason to talk you into the decluttering-topic is the big point of this book: YOU deserve a life where you just think: Wow, okay, I never thought that would ever be possible. In your living space, where you sleep, where you rest, where you spend time with your family and friends, and where you cook...it's really super important that you feel great at home.

Again, I don't know what level you graded yourself on the spoke of the living space on the wheel of life. It could be that you live in a really shitty place and can't afford another apartment, or live in the biggest mansion. Either way, you can feel great or desperate. And either way, you definitely have stuff to declutter.

The presents you've received, the really ugly ones that you hate to have on display but, you display them anyway because that's what's expected, right?

The things you've bought and don't use because you don't like them, don't actually need them, they don't fit, don't whatever...

The huge pieces of furniture you don't even realize are there anymore because you're so used to them, but if you're honest: You hate them.

I'll stop my list. Let's get to work, okay?

Decluttering is a really effective stress-reliever. At first, it's a real effort to start, but as soon as you get the hang of throwing things out of your life, you'll see that it feels freaking amazing! Don't believe me? Prove me wrong! Start anyway.

"Yeah, let's start, but HOW?"
Have you heard of Marie Kondo, the Japanese lady who wrote a worldwide bestseller about decluttering? She

currently has a Netflix show, where you can learn about her system of HOW to tackle even really, really overwhelming mountains of stuff. I read her book and always use it with my mastermind- and coaching-clients because her trick is so easy and a really good one. (It's not specifically designed for tough guys, but if you are one of those, you can keep this a big fat secret that you used the method of a tiny, little Japanese lady to get to the point where you're just amazed by your living space.)

Ready?

The short version: You go through ALL YOUR STUFF, take every single item in your hands, and ask yourself: Do I like this? Does it make me feel good? Marie Kondo asks: "Does it spark joy?"

> **"Are you crazy, Miss Sakata? Do you really think I'm going to wander through my house, hold my stuff and ask, 'Does this spark joy?'"**

Yep!

Miss Kondo suggests you start with one category, work your way through that pile, then go on to the next.

She tells you to start with your clothes. That's an easy one to tackle. Maybe you have tons of clothes, maybe only a few. Either way, get EVERYTHING out and into one big pile. Yes, even the snowboard jacket from the attic and clothes you have in your garage—just get them all OUT and throw them in the middle of your living room or bedroom. It can be overwhelming to see the sheer amount of clothes that you own, and to realize that you use only 20% of them—or even less.

Now is a good opportunity to clean out your closet (since it's empty), and then go to the mountain of clothes and start at the top of the pile. Take this t-shirt and ask yourself: Does it spark joy? If you don't dare to say something stupid like that, you could ask: Does it make me happy or feel good?

Don't ask: Does this fit me? Shall I wear this again? Is it still good? That's the trap of keeping things just because we "should", or because your mother told you to buy this, or your wife bought it for you.

Does it make you happy? Yes or no? Or maybe?

The Yes-pile goes back into your closet.

The No-pile goes to the thrift shop or homeless shelter, or wherever you can make a ton of people happy with your clothes you don't want anymore.

The Maybe-pile is actually the No-pile—because come on, if you don't make it to the yes-pile, you're OUT! (So true everywhere in life, right?)

I have a long-sleeved t-shirt from the biker-brand Fox that Ken wore all the time when we met back in 2001 in Japan. I love this shirt. He didn't want it anymore, but I wanted it. It's now twenty years old, there are holes in the sleeve cuff, it's too wide, and it's just a worn-down t-shirt. I use it as a pajama, and I feel great wearing it. All the memories of our road trips and camping nights at the beach on an island called Sadogashima are intertwined with this t-shirt. It sparks a ton of JOY for me, and I'll keep it until it falls apart.

That's why I like Marie Kondo's approach so much. It doesn't tell you to only keep the good and throw out the old and shabby things. It teaches you what you love and what you WANT, and that's the big question we're solving on so many levels throughout this book: What do I want? Once we know what we want, we can go get it!

Don't think that you can delegate this work. YOUR stuff is YOUR stuff, and only YOU can sort it out. You are also NOT allowed to throw things away that belong to other people in your household. The things of your spouse, your kids, your grandmother (if she's still alive) are NOT your business.

You might be thinking, "Yeah? Well, tell my lady that she should stop throwing my old beloved t-shirts away without even asking me!"

Oh, I will, for sure! Just leave this book lying around!

Ken and I have always had our own room—even when we only had an apartment with a living room, kitchen, bathroom, and two bedrooms. We decided which room is assigned to whom and created a golden rule: The other is not allowed to comment about anything in this room. Decoration, furniture, pictures on the wall... it's MY room or HIS room. MY room was our office, and I had a ton of pictures of our friends and family on the wall. I took the closet for both of us into my room, so I got to choose the design at IKEA. Ken's room was our bedroom, and besides the bed he had some locker-style furniture I don't really like, but hey... no comments allowed.

We still live by this rule, even now that we have a bigger apartment. Mika, our daughter, has her room and is the boss lady in there. The living room, hallway, kitchen and bathroom are middle ground space. Every new thing in there has to be approved by the democracy of our family. That's why we have a really bright, really bling-bling lamp from the hardware store in our hallway. I got outvoted. (It's a very, very ugly lamp, just so you know...)

When I started Marie-Kondoing our living space, I started with my closet (as you are, yes?), and I even folded the t-shirts and sweatshirts as she recommended. She says to put them upright, folded in little squares, into your drawers. That way you can see all your t-shirts right away. No piles are hiding the ones on the very bottom. I guess you still know the good old days of CD-shops? Shuffling through the rows of CDs of your favorite music style was so cool, and you could go really fast, right? That's how I feel about my drawers. It looks like a neat CD-shop. First, Ken commented that this is a stupid new thing to do (he is the laundry chief in our household, so he's putting away the super, neatly folded clothes)! And a week later, when I checked something in his closet, I saw that he had applied the CD-store-style to his t-shirts, too...ha!

Back to you, my friend! I hope you consider me as your friend. It would be a great honor, man, and I think if you hated me, you wouldn't be reading this damn book anymore, right?

I think you are just the greatest guy for trying and using all these new things! The changes in your life will amaze you, for sure. Who did it? YOU did it! High five and let's move on!

So, you worked through your pile of clothes, and only kept the things you love. Check!

Then, you put everything in the YES-pile back into your closet. If possible, avoid having a lot of boxes in your garage. Keep only the special jackets, ski pants, and chest waders somewhere else other than your closet. Ken's are hanging in the attic, and every time I go up there, I think that someone is hanging there, and it freaks me out.

You won't use the clothes in these boxes anyway. Also, if you have a storage-place, don't put clothes there. No way. You will not go there and think, "Oh, I'll wear this t-shirt today." Am I right?

Take away the carloads of clothes you don't want anymore. Don't let them sit in plastic bags in your hallway, okay? Out is out, and then you'll feel the greatest feeling of accomplishment. I swear, the energy will be different in your home after everything unwanted is gone!

Yes, we're only done with your clothes, but now you know how this works!

Marie Kondo tackles books next. Are you a big reader and have hundreds of books? Do you not even have one? Whatever your situation, you just apply the same question: Does this book make me happy? Does it spark joy?

I like to write a nice message into books I don't want anymore, and leave them somewhere in public. On a bench, in a subway, or in McDonald's. Finding a book without a message is nice, but finding one with a message from YOU is super cool! You can make someone's day, or change his or her life for the better with just your little note and the book. Will you try this? Wouldn't hurt, right?

Now you only have books you like on your shelves. Awesome!

Next is paperwork. All the manuals of any machine in your house, tax files, insurance-things. It depends on how long you have to keep this kind of stuff. By law, in Switzerland, it's ten years. After that, you can shred these files you will never look at anyway. Do you have loads of paper piling up everywhere?

My father turned eighty-one last year (2020). He has an office with paper piles so high, you would laugh out loud if you would enter his room. He has a system though, and he can find any article from a newspaper he kept from 1992. He was always our Mr. Google when we were still in school. Hey, I grew up without the internet! Ken was so shocked when he saw my father's office for the first time, and he always tells me that my messy style is inherited. I agree that I can't change, it's in my genes! My daddy would never declutter his office, because NOTHING in there is "clutter" in his opinion.

How about you? Would this be the greatest change for you to go and get rid of tons of paper in your living space? Go, go, go, and do it. For YOU. If you have a family, they'll be delighted if you get rid of these piles. The joy-question is lame here—I know you don't have sentimental feelings about your old tax files. Simply ask yourself: Do I need to keep this?

- **Clothes - done!**
- **Books - check!**
- **Paper piles - yep!**

Now let's tackle the kitchen! If you know that you have some boxes full of kitchen tools, silverware and tableware in your garage, bring them in and throw them on the pile too (gently, of course).

"The kitchen is NOT MY BUSINESS."

Oh, really? I'm so sorry. But could you help the person who is responsible for it? Anyway, a clean kitchen where every Tupperware box has a matching lid, all your nice frying pans have no scratches, and the fridge is clean is just the best feeling ever.

The mission is easy again: Does this coffee mug make you happy? No! You hate it, and you never use it, so throw it away or bring it to the thrift shop. Maybe someone else will totally love it! Remember, don't throw away the ugly mug that belongs to your teenager (or someone else). Only YOUR things. If a decluttered clean kitchen is just not at all your priority, guess what? YOU choose to do it or not. It's up to you.

There is a checklist for you on the book-bonus page www.joyismycompass.com/bookbonus where you can check off the different things to go through. Check it out if you want to go for it. It makes this huge, "all the things" category easier to go through.

Imagine again how you will feel when you enter your place and think: "Oh my freaking God, this is MY HOME!"

When you enter a hotel room and are just in awe of the niceness of this place... do you think it is impossible for you? No! Nothing is impossible! Just do it, man. If you watch T.V. for hours or scroll through social media for days, put your priorities in line and go and take care of your living space!

The last pile is sentimental things. You might be a collector; you might have little things, keepsakes you think you CAN'T ever throw away. Here comes the handy question again: Does it make you happy? Don't keep anything out of obligation. Don't put any gifts on display only when aunt so and so or this or that friend is coming over. This is YOUR space, and if they can't cope with you disliking what they gifted you, that's NOT your problem. Period.

"I will hurt their feelings."
NOT your problem. I prefer to be honest and tell the truth in a nice way: "Oh, that's nice, but I actually can't use this. Would you mind giving it to someone who really needs it?"

Do you think I'm rude? I think it's easier to say that right away instead of making things up until they've hopefully forgotten about it.

Just keep things you love. I'm very bad at letting sentimental things go, but if you wait long enough, you might think, "Why the hell did I keep this for so long?" Then it's easy to throw it away.

If your apartment or house is just a DREAM after going through all the corners and categories, don't forget your basement or your attic or garage or garden house or storage place. When you remember all the stuff you have there, you'll always think: "Shiiiit, in my storage, are fifteen huge boxes hanging around, and I don't even know what's in there..." So find out! And clean it out.

You can't hide your things—you are connected to all of them. I know that sounds witchy, but I really deeply believe this: Everything you own is connected to you, and if there are a ton of things in your life you own, and you don't even like them, they suck away your energy.

In the house where our shared apartment was, there

was a huge, super old, wooden attic, and every apartment had a compartment to put away their things. Swiss people normally have their ski equipment and other items which are only needed in a certain season up there.

People had been moving in and out of our apartment for the past ten years. I joined after five years. By then, the attic was full of random stuff from the guys and girls who had already moved out long ago. In front of all these lockable compartments, there was quite a big space that was supposed to be empty, common ground, from which we could all access the awesome rooftop terrace.

Well, this space at first only had some random items lying around, but over the years, it had piled up. The landlord of the house got really pissed by this and wrote a letter to each tenant, asking that we take our stuff and put it into our compartments; otherwise, it would get chucked out.

The result was: Everyone decluttered their compartments, and threw everything ON the pile. It was a gigantic mountain of furniture, carpets, books, sports gear, planks for flooring, ... an absolutely enormous pile. At first, we laughed. Then we got into thinking mode. Three of six apartments were shared, so basically, we were the bad guys in this game. We estimated that if this pile has to be carried down five floors without an elevator and be thrown away, it could be very, very, very expensive... Our feeling of being oh so clever quickly faded. So, we agreed on a Saturday when all of us, seven guys and two girls, would carry all this garbage down, ready to load into a gigantic trash truck that we booked through the city of Zurich. We worked for eight hours. Nine people. That would have ruined us if we had had to pay this. We had lots of fun combined with lots of swearing, but the attic was CLEAN after that. The pile outside of our house looked even bigger than it had underneath the roof with all the wooden beams. Not long after we finished, the first trucks pulled up, and they carried some of the furniture away. Our pile looked like an anthill full of people looking through the stuff. The number of things got smaller, until finally only the garbage was left. At night, we realized that others also wanted to take advantage and arrived with carloads of stuff themselves... we had to pay per quarter-hour for the loading time, so we weren't at all interested in the garbage mountain to get bigger again. We chased them away, and Ken, my husband, was awake all night doing the samurai-ninja job to get rid of the enemies. In the end, we paid only 80 bucks to get rid of everything, and we had such sore muscles from all the stair climbing. But I tell you, that feeling of finally having dealt with this stupid attic full of shit, that was amazing!

I hope that you are super motivated now to do whatever needs to be done, to change your living space to the way that makes you super happy, super proud, and super comfortable. That's the goal of all this work. Of course, it depends on your starting point as to how hard that will be. If you're in any way similar to my dad and me, you have a ton of things to work through. If you do not own so much stuff, you'll be done in a few days...or even hours?

Don't forget to decorate your space in the way you love it. If you didn't pay any attention to extras like decoration, think of what you would love to build-buy-create to make your space your OWN! This is not reserved for the ladies or professional designers. You know yourself what style you like, so get it into your home. If you live together with awesome people like your wife and kids, have a cool conversation about every room and how you could make it more comfortable, more unique, more personal, and maybe—if you don't cringe at this word—more beautiful! Did you cringe? Why is that? Use another word then, but please, consider yourself the VIP of your life. You deserve nice and beautiful things which bring you joy and make you happy.

When you are done with all this decluttering and decorating, throw a party to celebrate you and your space with as many or few people you'd like. This was a great effort, maybe also a team effort with your family? Either way, you should own the fact that you are a superstar, and you are fully in your power. Say thank you to YOU, because only reading a book doesn't change anything. Actually doing the things the author is trying to persuade you into doing, that's really great. I'm talking about you and me here. Congratulations, man! I'm celebrating YOU!

4

“IF YOU CARRY JOY IN YOUR HEART,
YOU CAN HEAL ANY MOMENT”

CARLOS SANTANA

CHAPTER FOUR

DECLUTTERING INSIDE

GET RID OF THE OLD SHIT

Now that you have a great space to live in where you feel like the king that you are, let's dig even deeper. This chapter might be a bigger challenge for you than the last one, but as I always tell you, it's so worth it. You don't have to tell anyone that you are doing these things. You might think you are not very manly because men don't do shit like this, but I know a lot of really nice, really tough, and really successful guys who do this and swear by it: It's journaling. Writing. Writing stuff down. For yourself.

I know I forced you to journal in the first chapter already... did it hurt? I didn't think so. Thinking about the important things in life AND writing them down is powerful. Really powerful. It can be a game-changer, the tool you never thought of that would make everything better in your life!

"C'mon, are you kidding me? A game-changer? Pen and paper should be a 'game-changer'...?"

Yes! Game-changer. Your thoughts are creating your reality!

"Is that so? Yeah?"

YES! Think of a situation: You're at the airport, waiting for your flight. It's delayed, and finally, there is an announcement that it's canceled. This information can cause severe stress and anger for one person, but another guy stays super calm and relaxed. Another guy, maybe you, is just so pissed off—and you're thinking, "AGAIN? Things like this always happen to me!"

What makes the difference between these three gentlemen? Same information, super different reaction... yes, it's only what they—what YOU—think.

I like situations like this. You can't change anything about the canceled flight, but you can think of all the options you have right now. Jens Corssen, the guy I always listened to while I worked on my thousands of salad-dressing bottles, suggests coming up with many options for any given situation that you dislike or struggle in. Not only three, because those are the most obvious ones, but eight options or more...let's go with ten! After five possibilities, what else could you do, or how else can you react? I know you'll get really creative. If you can stay in a good mood, you WIN anyway. I mean, a canceled flight is usually just very inconvenient, but doesn't cause any harm, right? Most situations that make us angry are totally up to us. We decide whether we want to react angrily or stay calm and in a happy mood.

"Oh, come on. You're getting on my nerves, little lady!"

First of all, I'm not little. I'm 178 cm (or five feet, eight inches) tall, and you should know me by now. I want to help you create a life you are blown away by, okay? For this reason, you need to go deep, and we have to talk about feelings, okay? I won't tell anyone, so if you don't tell, no one will ever find out. BUT, you will be different. You'll have a better mood (that's not so bad, right?), have better connections with your loved ones, and get along better with the people you meet on the street. You'll be more successful because a guy who brings a good mood with him connects well with others and is the best player in any company. Success will follow this JOURNALING SHIT, FOR SURE!

Can I talk in this chapter in my swishy way? Don't get me wrong: I don't think at all that showing your feelings and talking about them makes you, in any way, less masculine! Let me tell you, there is great power behind doing things your way, not caring what others think about you, and being all-in with your heart, your feelings, and your strength.

Let's go and get your superpower, my hero, shall we?

Your thoughts are super powerful and super important. Your thoughts determine how you react to ANY situation. Right now, you hear and see something, and your thoughts go wild. Instead, you could judge, evaluate, and then decide what your reaction should be.

If you can control and choose your thoughts, you are fully in control of your reactions, and that's really cool. For example, if someone calls you an asshole, you could:

1. Freak out
2. Call him or her whatever nice words you have in your vocabulary
3. Punch him or her in the face
4. Start a bar fight
5. Breathe and count to ten
6. Ignore this person
7. Ask: "Why are you calling me an asshole? Explain it to me!"
8. Say: "Oh, that's a nice thing to say. Are you always this friendly?"

9. Walk away, because you don't want to waste any of your treasured lifetime with people calling anyone an asshole. "Bye... have a good one!"
10. I don't have any more suggestions.

Stupid example? You can take ANY situation in your life and check in with yourself: What do I think about this, why do I react like this, and what are my ten options now? At work, at home, with your friends or with your neighbors. You always have options, and you can always choose how you want to react.

Can I start journaling now with you? Did you buy a notebook for all the wheel of life thoughts? Aah, you didn't even start to write your ideal day and the BE-DO-HAVE and the other exercises? Are you kidding me? Go and do this work, or throw this book away right now. Nothing will change in your life if you stay in spectator-mode and never go into ACTION-mode!

Okay, if you don't have a notebook (no need for unicorns and hearts on the cover, there are very nice, simple designs or unicolored ones out there too!), take a pen and some paper NOW.

(Yeah, I'm still the bossy, annoying teacher... sorrynotsorry! Oh, and if you have a journal and did all the exercises and you're thinking, "Why are you yelling at your good student?" I don't mean you. I have to get the students in the back on board the ship too, and I know that they need several attempts to get into gear...so just ignore me talking with them, okay? Thank you for your understanding!)

Write down all the situations in your life where you get or got angry (within seconds or where it built up over weeks), pissed, sad, stranded, mad, helpless...the situations you hate to be in, the situations where you would like to disappear or punch everyone...you know your life, write everything down!

Now, for every situation, think of ten options of how you could react differently than you usually do. Include the options you normally fall into, like getting really angry or getting really quiet, and then think of other options for the rest of the ten.

This might seem simple, but it's not. These situations occur all the time in your life; otherwise, you wouldn't have written them down. So, now your "catalog" of reactions will be in your mind the next time it happens again. Maybe you can't implement your other brilliant options right away. Still, now you're already in thinking mode, instead of just reacting instinctively the same way as always. This will change things, man. This will have a huge impact on your life, I swear!

It's like a workout. You don't see results right away, but over time, you're building your thought-muscle and reaction-muscle how YOU WANT. You choose! Choosing is always so much more powerful than just reacting automatically "because I just am that way." You are not directed by the circumstances; YOU are the boss of your thoughts and actions!

The good thing is that you have written down your vision already. You know what your dream life looks like, that's so good! But before we get there, step by step, I'd like to continue with the decluttering of thoughts, behaviors, and situations that you are in right NOW. Working through the ugly or sad or grinding side of life is not easy, but it is so worth it! Getting rid of what doesn't serve you anymore is very powerful, and in your future vision, you are a powerful guy, right? Powerful, self-confident, fit, healthy, strong, free, loved...what else? Let's get rid of everything that is not helping you become this superhero, which is already waiting inside you to get out!

Have you heard of Jesse Itzler? I'm sure your lady or future girlfriend knows his wife, Sara Blakely. She's a self-made billionaire (Yep! That's why you probably know her, too). I found Jesse through Sara's Instagram account, and you should definitely follow him (and her) too. I love how he creates his life with personal challenges (like running one hundred-mile races), how he spends time with his family with four kids, how independent he and Sara are in their relationship together, what a strong couple they are, AND how he treats his gang of friends. Check him out, you'll love him!

Jesse has a really cool TED Talk (I'll post the link for you on the book-bonus page www.joyismycompass.com/bookbonus, but you'll find him on Google too!) where he speaks about the happiness meter. No, don't roll your eyes, LISTEN!

He says: Imagine you put your whole life into a gigantic mixer. You blend together all the areas of your life. He calls them buckets: Family, Wellness, Business, Important Causes, Friends. I use the wheel of life, but it's the same way of thinking your life through. So, you throw all of your buckets into this blender. What number would you rate your overall life between one and ten? Everyone wants a ten, right? But that's "too much," "too perfect" because this, that and the other thing is not working/not yet fulfilled/sucks/...

Fill in the blanks! What made you back out from your initial ten? Catch these thoughts and write them down. Maybe you had a really big, fat, Aha-moment here?

Something like this:
"Yeah, it's my relationship with my lady. We're always fighting, and it's exhausting."

"Shit, I just hate my job. I don't want to work there anymore, but I'm scared that I'll never find a job I like, so I'd rather stay in this shitty job."

"Hmmm, I just don't have enough money. I'm living paycheck to paycheck, and I buy things I can't afford with money I don't have."

What's on your list? Write. It. Down!

Tada! Changing these things in your life and resolving them is the to-do list for your happiness. Easy? Not at all? But you can do it!

The first thing you need is awareness, and you have that now. Thank you, Jesse! I love this tool so much; I always use it in coaching and in my VIP-Mastermind. You should hear them say, totally amazed: "Wow, that's it? That's what's missing for having a ten out of ten?"

I know you did a lot of work already with your personal wheel of life, but this trick concentrates EVERYTHING in your life into a blender, and the insight can be mind-blowing. By the way, I also have male coaching clients, badass guys, who own the fact that they want to change something in their life. And they do! They pay a lot more than the price of this book (which you might have found on the coffee table in your living room? That was the secret procedure I told the ladies to get you to read this book...shit, now you found out...). But YOU can change your life just by reading these pages AND taking action. Will you? Are you all-in? Look at your list of things that should change to make your life a ten out of ten.

Maybe there is even more: What is it that you DON'T want any more in your life? It's like with the physical things you threw out. You can get rid of thoughts, behaviors, reactions, moods, habits, but also people. Getting rid of people? Duh, you're not killing anyone, but kicking the people out of your life who are only dragging you down, making you crazy, criticizing you constantly, you name it, is a good thing. They don't deserve a place at your table.

It works exactly the same with habits. Habits that make you angry, moody, tired, or sick don't deserve to get any of your time or energy. They have to GO! Of course, only if you want them to. You can keep anyone and anything in your life because you choose so, even though you know it's not good for you. You are completely free, and a grown man. This is good to hear from time to time, right? You're the captain of your ship!

Let's write a list of everything you can think of that would be so much better OUT of than IN your life!

I'll write a list of options for you; you choose what hits home for you. After that, you can write your personal list, okay?

- **Watching four hours of T.V. every day instead of creating your own company...there's an idea that always tumbles through your mind, but you don't grab it**

- Playing video games for hours, instead of taking care of your family by creating quality time with cool activities and places to go
- Smoking
- Hitting the snooze button fifty times and getting up late, so you only have ten seconds to get out the door for work
- Thinking you are a loser
- Judging yourself constantly for being too busy/lazy/fat/thin/old/young
- Calling yourself idiot/asshole/wimp/ (insert your favorite) a thousand times a day
- Feeling like you are failing in your job/business/relationship
- This "friend," who drags you down. Every time you see him or her, you feel like your energy is sucked out of you
- This "friend," who constantly criticizes you and tells you how to do things

"Are you kidding me? Am I going to be a saint after this book or what? I don't call myself a loser, I'm the BEST! I don't have shitty friends like this, hello! I can smoke and play videogames and watch T.V. as long as I want. YOU don't have to tell me to change for one second!"

Easy man! These are only possible points you might want to change or get rid of in your life. I told you a thousand times already, and I will tell you again and again: YOU choose. Not me. And NOT anyone else. No one has to tell you how to do things, how to live your life! Yes, your wife/girlfriend too should mind her own business, take care of herself, and not be managing you and telling you what to do.

Your parents brought you into this world, thank you so much, but now you are your own boss, and you can choose what you want. They don't have to tell you what to do for a living or whom you should marry.

Do you have other people you love, but you don't like it when they're bossing you around?

You're pointing at ME? No! I'm not one of them! I want YOU to think about what you want and don't want anymore. I want you to realize that YOU can DECIDE how you want to be and how you want to show up on the stage of life. For that reason, it's a great thing to think of the things and habits and people you don't want in your life anymore, and then CHANGE IT step by step!

You don't have to become a saint! You don't have to change a thing. But you have millions of possibilities to become the person you really want to be. No, you're not stuck. You just haven't decided yet that you WANT to change.

"Yeah, I tried to quit smoking, but it didn't work. I can't."

No way. You just don't want to quit smoking. That's all.

If you own this and say, "Okay, at the moment, I don't want to quit. So, I smoke." That feels so much better than playing some sort of a victim who can't do anything about this.

"Do or do not. There is no try."
~ Yoda

I literally know nothing about Star Wars, except for this Yoda quote that I love so freaking much!

Don't try to break your bad habits or try to stop doing things. Trying is losing already. Do it and stick with it, or don't do it and own it.

Breaking up with cigarettes is not as hard as breaking up with people, but it's the same way of looking at it.

"Oh man, I spent an evening with him again. I feel so freaking tired. He talked so much without asking me once how my game is going..."

Will you tell this friend that you won't have time for him next time he asks you to hang out? No? Yes? If you don't want to kick him out of your life, that's completely okay! Just knowing that it's okay to do it when the time is right sets you in a different place of power. Who knows—maybe your relationship will shift and become a really good one. I'm not at all saying that you have to kick every annoying person out of your life.

"I like some annoying people very much. I don't want to kick them out—I want them to CHANGE!"

Bad news:
You can't change anyone but YOURSELF.

Doesn't that suck?

As I told you earlier, I love the fact that you own YOUR thoughts, YOUR dreams, YOUR vision, YOUR action, YOUR mood. You are not responsible for anyone else but yourself. Isn't that a relief? You're not responsible for your friends, for your lady, not even for your kids. They are whole human beings who want to live life their way.

"No no no, I have to tell them what to do, when to do it, and how to behave."

Really? You could start today to treat them as your partners in crime, and SHOW them how to treat others, how to behave. For example, don't yell at little people that they should stop yelling! Try whispering in a very calm voice and show them how YOU live life. Or, for example, how you treat your tools and things very carefully and respectfully. They watch you ALL THE TIME, for sure. They watch how you treat their mother, your wife, or your girlfriend. That's how they learn about relationships and how to communicate. This applies not only to children—this book is not a parenting book, for sure.

It matters how you present yourself in your life. You have a big influence on EVERYONE around you. This example was with kids. How about your girlfriend, your wife, or the lady you dream about? Do you show your spouse the respect and love you want to get from her? Do you treat her how you want to be treated? What did your relationships look like when you did the looking-back exercise at one hundred years old? Are you doing things that way already, or is there loads of room for improvement?

Can we meet your future self again for a minute? Does he have time for us?

Can you imagine this? Just for fun! You'll gain a ton of insights. Imagine yourself in ten years, okay? So, you're not yet one hundred (I guess) but quite a bit further along than the present you. He is the best version of yourself. He has been very conscious about his decisions in the last decade! He did all these freaky exercises of this crazy Swiss woman, read a ton of other books, listened to inspiring podcasts, and then, he knew: "This is MY life. I can decide how to spend every day, be how I choose to be." He decluttered his home and his life and took action BIG TIME to create the life of his dreams. The big, fat vision was (and is still) clear!

Imagine your future self entering the coffee shop where we're meeting. Look at him! He looks so damn good: Healthy, radiant, full of energy, and just plain happy!

His energy is contagious. You somehow already feel better from just watching your future self enter the room.

"WOW! That's ME? In ten years?"

YES! This is you. Let's meet him and talk to him and learn about ALL THE THINGS he did, to get to the point in his life where he is obviously rocking it in a big way!

Imagine this scene, please. Don't shy away and think it's stupid! This is real, powerful stuff. I don't know your life, your circumstances, your dreams, and wishes, but HE does! And he's living them!

Shake his hand, or better yet, give him a big bear hug. Feel how strong and healthy his body is! He didn't do it overnight. He worked for this every single day. No, you don't have to become a gym person if you hate it there. You design your life on your terms, remember. So, if he is so strong and healthy and radiates power, he did it YOUR/HIS way, of course.

Feel how much he loves you! He's your biggest fan. Your fan from the future. He knows exactly what you're going through. He knows all your fears and your dreams. He loves you just the way you are now. You don't have to change to get his approval. He tells you how awesome you are, how big and small decisions will have a huge influence on you and your life right in the next weeks and months. You will not be the same person in even half a year. You are rocking it so hard!

Imagine that he sits down with us. Oh, shall I leave? I don't want to disturb your conversation at all! Let me throw in some questions you could ask him before I go, okay? It seems like an interview, but hey, you want to know all his secrets! His moves! His habits! His self-care, because it's super clear to you that this man takes very good care of himself. You are amazed that this is YOU!

Read through these questions. The first answers that come to your mind and imagination are the answers from your future self, okay? I know this sounds very, very weird, but hey, you are my hero because you are still reading! These kinds of mind-boggling exercises are soo damn helpful. You won't get your advice from ME, but from YOUR future self. Of course, you'll listen more to him. I get that, and I love that! He's your superhero. He's your role model. And that's exactly what I want him to be for you. HE can help you achieve more in the next six months than anyone else in your life. Isn't that cool? An imaginary friend that happens to be the best version of your future self in ten years.

Yep, you don't have to tell anyone! Yes, this can be your secret weapon! Yes, this is crazy, but you don't care, right?

If you are ready to get even crazier (although, I think it's not crazy but rather very cool), do the future-self meditation, which you can download on the book-bonus page www.joyismycompass.com/bookbonus.

During the meditation, you will meet your future self, as before, and be able to ask him questions. The helpful difference is that you are in a meditative state of mind, where your judging mind is "waiting in the corner" and not yelling mean comments all the time. That way you can experience the whole scene with an openness, which is such a cool experience. I do this meditation with all my clients, and it's crazy what they tell me about what they "experienced" and saw, like a movie with clear pictures and super practical insights. On top of the advice you get from your future self, you FEEL his energy, and that can be "life-changing" (I know this word is so overused, but sometimes, it's just that!) You gain more motivation to change your life through this, more than with any other advice from anyone. So, did I convince you to do the meditation? YOU decide.

You can gain great insights by just answering the questions, which I still didn't give you! Now it's time to fully go into this scene of you and your powerful future self, sitting in this coffee shop and talking about life. Maybe he doesn't want to spoil your experience and will keep some secrets to himself. Just ask anyway!

Here are some questions to ask him:

- How did you even start changing your situation?
- If you were me right now, what would be your next important step?
- I'm totally overwhelmed with making all these changes. I want to stay where I am, but hey, I see YOU, and I'm amazed...tell me, how did you do it?
- What would you do in my situation with (insert challenge/issue/problem)?
- Shall I keep contact with (insert the person you are not so sure about still keeping in your life)?
- How shall I interact with my parents, who I love, but who drive me crazy?
- Where do you live now?
- Are you in a relationship? With whom?

How wonderful, if you are in love now and it's brilliant, or difficult, and now you hear that in ten years you're still together. Since your future self looks so damn great, he must have a blast with his lady, yes? Isn't that soothing? Isn't that the greatest motivation to take care of your relationship in a very deliberate way? You can do this! Step by step. We'll get to this in the next chapter.

If you are single now and you're looking for an awesome lady to rock your life with, you will surely hear from him that you/he found your soulmate. She's a really cool woman, who is absolutely thrilled that she found YOU! Isn't that nice!?

If you are single now and you don't want to change anything about this situation because you love to be on your own, GREAT! I'm pretty sure that your future self will tell you stories about how amazing his life is, with or without a woman in it.

Ask any question off the top of your head and think of the first answer that comes to mind. I told you that's a lot easier in the meditation, so just TRY IT. It's fun and free, you don't have any excuses.

- **Do you like this?**
- **Are you freaked out?**
- **Was that the last straw?**

I think that by now you're pretty used to me and my "craziness," so I'm not worried. You shouldn't be worried either. It's just a book with words printed on a piece of paper. You are a free man, and you can do and think whatever you want.

BUT your future self was pretty awesome, right? Intriguing? I hope so!

He'll motivate you when you are down! He'll tell you, show you that everything will work out perfectly, even though it might seem impossible at this very moment. He's your buddy, your partner in crime, and if you want to have him in your life, just think of him as your invisible coach. You can have him by your side in any situation, and ask for help and advice. Remember the airport-situation and the ten options we discussed at the beginning of the chapter? He can help you in any stress-situation to find ten cool options, OR he just can tell you what to do—since he already resolved this situation in the past (I know this is crazy time-traveler-shit, but so much fun and it's a tool I love).

So, if you're fighting with someone, remember your future self, and hiss to him in your mind, "WHAT should I say or do right now?"

You might be stunned at what enters your mind: "Walk away, this is not worth it! GO!"

Maybe you're fighting with your spouse, and you are so mad.

He might whisper, "Now is the time to just go over and take her in your arms and hug her dearly!"

"WHAT? Hug her? NOW? She pisses me off!"

"Trust me!"
I suggest making a deal with your future self that you promise to take his advice without exception. How can he coach you if you don't listen? If you have the power to get new inputs, like hugging your lady in a fight instead of handling the situation like you always would, how freaking powerful is that? Just listen to the voice in your

head. It's him, and you know him. He's doing really well, and you want to be like him, so it might be a really good idea to just execute what he's telling you to do.

Hugging an upset person, be it your wife, your girlfriend, your angry child, or your friend, is so powerful. You can use your masculine power, your strength, and your whole body to help release the anger and the tension. You're not weak by hugging instead of fighting. You are changing the narrative of the world. You own your power and use it in the most loving way. I like your future self for this hint! He's a great man, and so are you!

If you think, "No way I'll EVER become that superhero", stop this limiting train of thought right in its tracks. Just ask your coach, AKA your future self, loads of questions every single day in every little moment of stress or insecurity. By building up this relationship with him, you WIN YOUR LIFE! Yes, it's all in your mind (and heart), and it doesn't hurt, and you can stop it anytime, but man, don't miss out on this. He can help you with the challenges you have to conquer to fetch a ten on the happiness meter too. And quit smoking, if that's what you want to do. He's your man. He's your coach. He's your inspiration! He's your motivation!

Do the meditation too, okay? Deal? You are my hero. Thank you for spending all this time with me. Thank you for being so open-minded and "crazy" to try these tools and exercises. You're doing it for you! And you will see the changes rolling in for SURE. And these changes are going to be AWESOME!

Let's jump into the next chapter (after you've done every exercise so far...otherwise, you're NOT ALLOWED to turn the page)! You did all the decluttering, your house is just a dream, you love your living space. You kicked some habits and some people out of your life, and you have a deal with your future self to listen to him so that upsetting situations can actually work out in a very positive way. That's you, right?

Yeah, I know, and I love that fact: You can do whatever you want, and no one has power over you, how you should think, what you should do, how you should act...that's all in YOUR hands, and this is the BEST thing! Do you agree?

The next chapter is all about self-care. Don't shrug. You saw your future self. He's in such good shape, physically and mentally. He's doing the right things at the right time, and that's what we'll talk about. Self-care is not reserved for women in spas. Self-care is not at all only about wellness and manicure and pedicure. It's about taking care of your body and mind and soul in a very individual, personalized way so that it suits YOU and no one else. Ready? Let's do this!

5

"LET YOUR JOY BE IN YOUR JOURNEY -
NOT IN SOME DISTANT GOAL"

TIM COOK

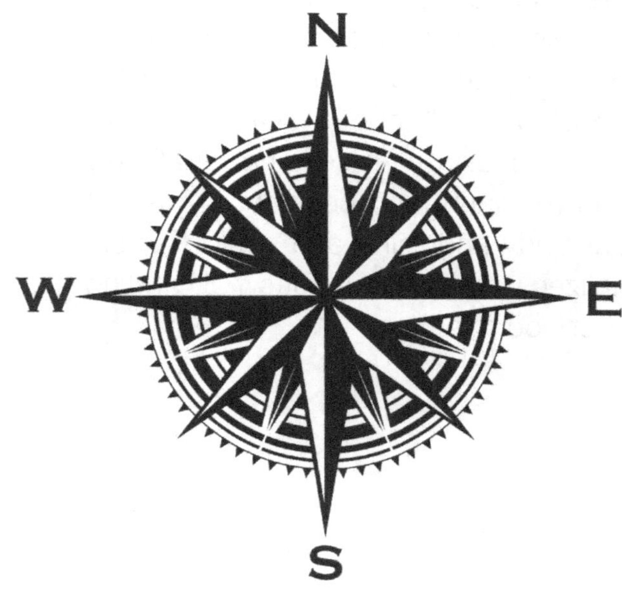

N
W
E
S

CHAPTER FIVE
SELF-CARE

YES SELF-CARE! STAY WITH ME!

I have eight questions for you. Just answer them right away without thinking too much, okay?

- Who do you trust the most?
- Who do you love to spend time with the most?
- Who knows all your secrets?
- Who knows your forbidden dreams?
- With whom can you discuss your Be-Do-Have list for hours?
- Whom do you love wholeheartedly?
- Who is the most important person in your life?
- Whom can you ask, "What's my next step?"

(If you answered "my future self" for the last question, I love you even more than before. Oh, come on. I can say that, no?)

Are these questions too airy-fairy for you? The answer is one name, so don't chicken out about them!

So, how many times did you answer with "ME"? Zero out of eight? Eight out of eight?

Did you even consider yourself as an answer to the questions?

"But I sound like an egomaniac if I consider myself as an answer!"

Really? I don't agree.

Of course, you love to spend time with your friends or your lady! But you are with YOU from your first breath until your last. You spend every second of your life with yourself, so, it would be really nice if you love to be with yourself, trust yourself, AND love yourself, right? Nobody knows that you're reading and implementing these things. You're just more and more aware of your power and how taking care of yourself is a really good thing. You have more energy, you are feeling good, you are happier, and with all that, you have more to give! Your personal and business relationships will benefit because, hey, it's just nicer to work together with a cheerful guy, than with a grumpy one. It's also nicer to live with a guy who has his shit together and takes care of his own needs.

Let's dig into this topic now from the practical side. This is something you DO every day. It's nothing philosophical.

No, you don't have to do awkward things you hate. Of course you don't! You are customizing this to your own needs and taste. You should know me by now!

We'll cruise through all the areas of your life and talk about what caring for yourself could look like for you. Shall we start with food this time? I mean nutrition. Nope, I won't call you out if you eat fast-food. I'm the biggest believer that if you enjoy your food to the fullest, it's doing you good. This means that you need to get super clear on what you WANT to eat, and then enJOY it without any guilt involved. What I also love to focus on: How does this food make you feel? I know, a feely question again, but hey, you are here to learn something new, right?

Think about your car, you give your car fuel, and of course, you don't put diesel in your tank if it needs gasoline. You check the oil frequently and just take really good care of your (beloved) vehicle. And if it's worn down, old, and doesn't work anymore for you. You buy a new one.

The thing is with your body: You've got only one. Buying a new one is not possible, and spare parts are hard to come by, so I think it's just the coolest thing to take care of your body. This is called self-care. Remember how your future self looked so damn good? He was fit and healthy and strong and radiant, and that doesn't come out of nowhere. Self-care should be fun and tailored to you; otherwise, there is no point. Life should be FUN and filled with adventure and joy. It should feel amazing. Okay, okay, you still can't stand sentences like this, right? Okay, I'll give you some extra time to get used to these rose-colored glasses. You'll get there, I promise!

FOOD. FUEL. GAS FOR YOUR ENGINE

For one semester, I was teaching food engineers about nutrition at the Zürich University of Applied Sciences. The schoolmaster asked me to create a new curriculum that would inspire and motivate these students about this topic. I began my research and decided soon after that it's just not possible for me to choose out of all the topics and tell them, "THIS is the truth, memorize it and pass a test." During my five years at university studying food science, the facts we were taught in nutrition changed 180 degrees, two times. First, fat was bad, but carbohydrates were good. Then, all these light- and low-fat products sprung up like mushrooms in the supermarkets. Later, carbohydrates became the EVIL thing to eat. Low carb, keto diet, blahblahblah... I'm a big fan of all these hypes...NOT!

As for my students, I decided to challenge them, and I had them read some books about nutrition. I ordered thirty books on Amazon: The Truth About Carbohydrates, Why Carbs Are the BEST for Your Body, Eat Only Fat and You'll Get Slim, and so on, all kinds of titles that totally disagreed with each other. Books about vegan, keto, Atkins, low fat, low carb, anything "low" or "high." Each student chose one book and held a presentation about the topic at the end of the semester. The bottom line of ALL these books is my food philosophy, and you will roll your eyes: YOU have to find out what is best for you. No expert, no guru, no one else but YOU can decide what's good for you.

"Oh cool, so I can drink six cans of beer every night and eat doughnuts for dinner?"
Of course, you can! You can do anything you want. No one can tell you to finish what's on your plate. No one can force you to eat broccoli or whatever it is you hate!

It's your choice what you eat and drink. Good for you! And who is helping you decide? The cool, radiant guy, who is so damn good looking and healthy as f**k! Do you know his name? He works for free, and he adores you and wants only the best for you. If you didn't see your future self smirking at you, you have to reread the last chapter.

Put him into your head and heart. Discuss with him, what you should choose to eat and drink, and after you've decided, you had better enjoy these doughnuts to the fullest and drink these beers with a smile!

Oh—he will not let you eat this kind of food? Poor you! Are you forced into more healthy choices? He has no mercy with your food habits? That's not my business, sorry...you have to deal with your desires to become THIS guy.

You could also drink five bottles of vodka every day and eat whatever you want from now on. But if you do that, maybe the plan with your one hundred-year-old self will not work out perfectly, and the radiant future self is gone with the wind.

You know what I want to get across: YOU decide ("Ronja, you've said that a thousand times..." I know, but it's so damn true, and we always forget, so, I'll say that a thousand times more, sorrynotsorry!). With the help of your future self, these decisions get easier and easier over time until it's a walk in the park. You'll sometimes treat yourself to "unhealthy" things, but it will be easy to stick with the food that you love AND is GOOD for your engine, for your mobile unit, which you've got for this lifetime.

Let's do some journaling, shall we? Get out your book and pen, mister!

Write a list of ALL your favorite dishes, products, and treats. Just EVERYTHING you love to eat! Don't forget your childhood favorites! Maybe it was your grandma's pasta Napolitana?

How many times did you eat food you love last week? Last month? You can write these numbers behind the items on your list. Check it out—you love Thai-curry so much, but you didn't eat it once last month...

Go through your list, together with your future self, and discuss the different meals and treats. Which one should you reserve for special occasions? Which ones do you want to push to the top ten? What could you add to the list, without making any compromises about liking the food you eat? What could you try that you've never tried before?

If you're done with your list, you can think about last week: Monday through Sunday. Write down everything, every meal and snack you ate, and the drinks you had. What gave your engine fuel last week? Did you choose things you love to eat, or did you just shove something into your mouth? This is an interesting investigation. There's nothing to be called out—just observe. Your new focus for choosing food shall be the new list you wrote down with your future self.

I'm deeply amazed by what our body is doing for us. I mean, you can stuff a Big Mac in your mouth, and the rest is fully automated!? Digestion cuts all the nutrients into the molecules, which then make their way from your gut into your blood. Your heart beats about 100,000 times per day. Isn't that exhausting? No! Fully automated. You don't ever have to think about your heart. Isn't that handy? MAN, your body is a miracle! And it's all fueled by what you throw into your mouth.

If you decide to take care of your engine and give it the best fuel, you might switch your food and drink choices. If you manage to eat and drink "with full appreciation" of what your body is doing for you, I guarantee that you'll find a healthy balance between all the things you love. Don't let your future self off the hook. He's your man. He can tell you what he would decide in this red-hot minute, and then YOU decide if you want to listen or not.

If you are in a relationship, and your lady is ALWAYS telling you what to eat, what to avoid, and hands you green smoothies every morning, which you can't stand, it's time to have a conversation. It's just not working this way. You feel (I imagine) like a little boy being pushed by his mom to eat this or that, and you throw a tantrum because you don't want to do what she's telling you. You want to decide YOURSELF what to eat or drink! Am I right?

She wants to help you, she wants to support you, and she most certainly wants to keep you healthy because she loves you and wants you to stick around for a long time. BUT, you have to decide on your own. This fight is not going to make things any better. You have to take full responsibility for your body, mind, and spirit. And she has to do that for herself, too! Of course, you can support each other. This would be super cool and fun after you've sat down (after you've done your own private personal journaling and investigation of HOW you want to change things) and talked with her. If she didn't do the exercises yet, do them together! Find your favorite meals, talk about what your future selves would suggest, and discover how you can implement this wisdom into a daily routine that is tasty (so damn important) and good for your bodies!

You don't have a lady at your side (did you buy this book by yourself? I love you!), and still you want to discuss these kinds of questions with a real human and not some freaky future-self imagination? Go you! Tell a friend about this book and discuss how you want to change things. He or she will be happy to join you, for sure, and would love to be your accountability partner.

What do you agree with? Eating more fresh food? Making things from scratch? No fast-food during the week? Going to a cooking class? (Choose a fun one, where cool guys like you are a perfect fit!) But hey, who needs a cooking class when there is YouTube? Choose the meal you want to eat, buy the ingredients, and just follow the instructions. Making yummy things is not difficult at all. Cooking is super easy if you just go for it.

When I would come home to my shared apartment after a party, it usually stank like crazy. You know why? Sometimes, there was something black (a former sandwich) in the oven, which was about to burn because it was dry like coal. My flatmate Peter loved to prepare food before he passed out in his bed, with the oven on full speed. He also was a professional pan-handle melter. Since he found our kettle disgusting (he could never explain why) he always boiled water in a pan for his instant noodles...but one day he left the pan on the stove and forgot about it, and as soon as the water was gone, the pan got roasting hot and the pan handle slowly melted. I told you I had lots of fun with the boys back then. Peter was an excellent cook, when sober, and he was even my best man at my wedding because he and Ken had become friends while living together. If you would have told me that this sandwich-burning, pan-handle-melting guy would be my best man in the near future, I would have punched you in your face! (Love you, Peter!)

So, cooking is not hard, just don't fall asleep, okay?

Try new recipes. Buy ingredients you've never heard of. Prepare loads of Thai-curry and freeze a bunch in freezer bags. Prepare loads of tomato sauce, pumpkin soup...whatever you like. This does not mean that you'll turn into a square.

This is the coolest thing you can do for yourself AND your family! You are making your own convenience food! Lots of people—I think you are one of them—think that preparing food takes too long and it's difficult and hard, so they pick up the fast-food they know or order pizza. My food is prepared very fast! Ken is even quicker at cooking than me. Recently he preheated the frying pan while checking the fridge for ingredients. I asked him, "What are you cooking?" He replied, cool as always, "I don't know yet!"

I'll share my super-easy, super-quick tricks, ok?

For me there are basically 4 types of sauces:

1. Soy sauce based, Japanese-Chinese-Asian type (hey, I'm married to a Japanese chef, I can tell you secrets!)
2. Tomato-based, Italian type
3. Curry-based, Indian-Thai type (not the same, I know... Japanese and Chinese are not the same, either, but the ingredients are similar)
4. White sauce, creamy-cheesy (Macaroni and cheese) type

Possible ingredients: Fresh onions, fresh garlic, soy sauce, sesame oil, rice vinegar, mirin (that's a fancy Japanese ingredient, which lasts forever and makes everything better. It's sweet rice wine), rice vinegar, and olive oil (or any oil).

I chop some onions and fresh garlic (crush the garlic underneath your cutting board. Getting rid of the husk is a walk in the park that way) and some veggies, the ones I have around. I don't like complicated recipes; I like to use what's in my fridge. I booked a weekly delivery of locally grown organic veggies (yes, very important to me) that miraculously appear on the windowsill of my kitchen every Wednesday morning. I love it. Sometimes I have to google what's in the box, as it's always a lucky bag. Have you heard of dinosaur kale? It looked freaking cool, like the skin of a reptile.

Whatever you find for FRESH veggies, chop them. I eat vegan, so tofu-cubes or chickpeas or beans are my protein. If you eat meat, just fry some (chicken, beef, pork) in a shot of olive oil, and eat it as a side dish. Fry the veggies until they are as tender or firm as you like. Mix everything together, throw some mirin and soy sauce in your frying pan. Add some drops of sesame oil and a little rice vinegar. Serve this mix on rice (you know how to cook rice, right? If not, google it!), and it's as good or even better than at an Asian restaurant. Isn't that cool?

You're a chef! If you think I'm stupid to think that a cooking class could take place in a book, head over to YouTube! There are really cool guys who tell you, step by step, how to cook fresh and super tasty meals. For me, that's the most important part that my food tastes super good. And I tell you: The lady in your life (or future lady in your life) will be THRILLED if you are her private chef. You don't have to serve a five-course meal. Just something fresh and tasty and cooked with love...wow, you'll make so many points on the scale. You won't regret that you've practiced in secret or with your friends!

Ah, you liked my written cooking class? You want to know how the Italian sauce works? Even easier than the Asian one:

The ingredients: Canned tomatoes, fresh garlic and fresh onions, olive oil, salt and pepper, a dried Italian herb mix (e.g. oregano, basil, thyme and rosemary), parmesan cheese (there are vegan versions out there if you want to impress your vegan crush), if possible some (cheap or expensive) red wine, and any pasta you like.

Chop the garlic and onions (yes, it will make you cry. I find it so funny, to stand in my kitchen with tears floating down. Mika, my daughter, uses her ski-goggles for eye protection; that works like a charm. Please, please send me a pic of you standing in your kitchen chopping onions, okay?). You don't have to have a specific technique, just chop and keep your fingers safe. Put some olive oil in a deep-frying pan, throw in the chopped onions and the garlic, fry them, pour some red wine over them (if you don't have wine, water is okay, too). Be prepared for a big whoosh, and let the wine evaporate for a while. Then add the tomatoes, and let this mix simmer (with the lid on, but a little open) on the lowest heat level for an hour, if possible. Add some Italian herbs. If you want to, add some fried minced meat and any veggies you like. Add salt and pepper until it tastes really good, and the sauce is ready. I always prepare a huge amount and freeze some portions—my own convenience food, as I told you. When you come home from work, you just need to cook pasta and heat the homemade pasta sauce...and this feels GOOD! Your future self is living that way, right? So why not start right away with this yummy lifestyle?

If you are still interested in a cooking class, please come over to my book-bonus page:
www.joyismycompass.com/bookbonus.

I have all the tips and tricks there ready for you, but I don't want to bother you with recipes in this book anymore, because Google and YouTube can help you much better than I can here. I just want to encourage you to learn how to cook. It's sexy, it's cool, and it's so damn tasty to eat your own meals. You can do it! And if you hate it, of course, you don't have to do it! Maybe you have the money to hire a chef to prepare meals for you the whole week? Make your food, your fuel, the gas for your body a priority!

You can train as much as you want, but your body's base is earned in the kitchen. They say 75% is what you eat and 25% how you move your body!

We've tackled the 75% now in this chapter. Just eat the best things you can find and ditch the crap. If you love sweets and junk food, eat it only on rare occasions and concentrate on fresh food made from scratch. You're not up to that? No problem. You decide! Nobody demands accountability of you (maybe your wife, but that doesn't work out, am I right?). Only YOU can decide what you WANT to do. Only you can change how you want to feed yourself. OWN your decisions. As I told you in the beginning: Eating super, unhealthy food with lots of pleasure and a huge smile on your face is much better for your body than shoveling it in your mouth with loads of guilt and shame. Our minds are powerful, and if you think it's healthy and makes you happy, that's what happens to be true. Cool, right? Do it your way, baby, and love your food and your body hard.

Let's go to movement, shall we?

MOVE YOUR VEHICLE

Are you a typical couch potato? Super sporty? Well trained? Do you go to the gym daily? Do you do loads of workouts per week? Have you never done any sports at all in your life?

I don't know what shape you are in, obviously. I don't know what your starting point is, but I know for sure though that EVERYTHING is possible. I'm sure you've seen the amazing videos, where guys lose two hundred pounds in two years (no quick diets, please!), and how they just decided to change, and so they did? I know that's easier said than done, but it is doable.

ANY fitness goal is a good one—and hey, you saw your future self. He's in great shape. So, ask him: What did you do? Then call him all the names you want, because you are so fucking jealous that he looks so good!

If you are already in the same shape as your future self, skip this paragraph, okay? This is for those of you who want to become fit. As I have been working more and more with people one-on-one in my coachings or in my masterminds, I have gotten to know a lot of people on a very deep level—their thoughts, wishes, fears, and struggles. Maybe you are a wise man already, but I was a very judgy girl for the longest time in my life. Now I'm better! Most of the time. For sure, I won't judge you if you consider yourself lazy or overweight or both or whatever. I just want to shake up your life and urge you to DECIDE! Decide to stay in front of your T.V. and ENJOY what you're doing. It's the same as with food. If you enjoy hanging around and not doing anything sportswise, that's a hell of a lot healthier than having a guilty conscience. Will staying in front of the T.V. for hours make you fitter, though? Probably not, if you don't have a home trainer or a rowing machine in front of the screen. I myself am a gym-hater, but I love to do workouts in my living room in the morning before my family gets up.

Think of movement that you really like. Hiking? Walking? Swimming? Yoga?

Don't judge yoga too quickly. You can try it secretly for yourself with a YouTube personal trainer. "Yoga with Adriene" is my choice, and she comes over to my home with a click, for free. I love her, but there are a TON of different trainers out there. If you search for "yoga men" you'll find very well-defined men teaching yoga. Try it! Yoga is good for your mind and body and for any level of fitness or flexibility.

You think yoga is from the devil? Okay, okay... (challenge yourself and do yoga for a week or a month, and ditch it once you're convinced that it really is from hell...but before you try it, you just don't know, right?)

Running? Now THAT'S from hell, in my opinion. But hey, all you need is some sneakers, and off you go. Start out running for some minutes and then walking for some minutes until you can run longer distances. If you want to get inspired to run, follow Jesse Itzler, the guy who talks about the "happiness meter." He's so much into running that I sometimes, almost, get the urge (for a second) that I might try this stupid sport again. Just for a second, though...

You don't need a list of all the sports you could start doing. Just choose something you like, which is FUN! Why should you do something you don't like? By doing the sport you like, you'll get in better and better shape—and hey, you have a personal coach who's looking so damn good: Your future self. Let him tell you what you should change - do - start. Martial arts? Water gymnastics? You laugh at that, but your joints will love you for dropping some pounds in the water.

Just shake up the cells of your body and DO SOMETHING...or do nothing with a smile, that's okay, too. Your choice. If you think eating healthy AND doing sports is way too much, then choose healthy eating first. Balanced food has much more of an impact on your body than eating trash and doing sports. DEAL?

SELF-CARE IN RELATIONSHIPS

Is this going places you don't want to think about? Stay with me! Relationships can be the most beautiful thing in our lives or the most devastating... and everything in between.

I don't want to go into psychology. I want to ask you some questions again: What do you want in your relationships? How do you want to be treated? How do you want to treat others? What do you want to say to your loved ones, but you never did up to now because of thoughts like, "This is not manly enough. I don't want to talk about feelings! I'm not good at communication, so I better say nothing."

Can we please talk to your future self for a minute? He figured out the way he wants to interact, communicate, and show love, appreciation, and affection to the people around him. He knows his boundaries. He says what he needs in a relationship. He knows what he wants in a relationship. He made it very clear what is a no-go for him, and he knows that the rules in relationships are always a two-way thing. But first, you have to know what's important to YOU.

Journal it out! Write everything down that you wish for in your relationships, a wish list for every important relationship you have. With your spouse, with your kid(s), with your neighbors, with your boss, with... Ah, you don't have a spouse? Well, you know what? It's the BEST thing to attract the best lady into your life by writing down what you wish for. How she will be, how you'll be. Write it down in the present tense, as if it is already your reality.

Thank you for my wonderful lady (you wouldn't write "wonderful?" WHY NOT!?). Thank you for my girl, she is so cool. She knows what she wants. She has her own dreams. She's powerful. She is so self-confident that I know I don't have to care for her or heal her. She takes responsibility for her own shit, I take responsibility for mine, and together we are a dream-team. Thank you for my relationship with her, which feels so EASY! It's just cool. We are cool together. She loves me just how I am and doesn't want to change me. I want her to be herself and will change with her, together. We are a team. She's my gang. She accepts my friends. I can go out without her, she can go out without me. We trust each other. That's so cool, and totally stress-free. Man, thank you for my girl—she's just pure gold!

Is that too much to ask for? I don't think so.
Is this not at all your personal dream of a romantic relationship? Write YOUR version!

Think it through. Dream of your perfect lady. Maybe you want the traditional thing: I'm a strong guy, and I will protect my little lady. Or maybe you prefer an equal, eye to eye relationship. I prefer that we support each other out of strength, not weakness. I don't think men and women have to be the same—we are different, anyway—but I believe in being responsible for only yourself. What she does is her business. I believe in trust. I believe in supporting each other's dreams. I believe in being kind to each other. I believe in surprising my husband, having fun together, celebrating life, feeling good, and having a damn good time!

This applies to any relationship. I believe in having fun at work with your team, with your boss. No, life is not always a bowl of cherries, but why not bring a little lightness into the daily grind? Surprise your work colleague(s) with a fun or kind sticky note, or with a cool prank (not a mean one).

Relationships are everywhere, and YOU decide how to show up for them. For that, you have to know what you want. But as you are a journaling pro by now, you are writing down every thought on relationships, and I tell you, just by doing this, your relationships are gonna change for the better!

Talk to a homeless guy and buy him some good food. This man will love you for respecting him as a human being, because they don't often have the chance to talk to somebody just in a normal way.

"Is this self-care, Ronja?"

I think YES! Knowing what you want and communicating it exactly because you know that you are fully responsible for YOU and nobody else—that's powerful!

It's about being aware of who you are, how you show up, and how you treat your people. You decide. Decide wisely. You'll feel good for sure. And hey, if your relationships feel bad, if your personal rules are violated or dismissed, you have to speak up. If the other person listens, you can discuss how you want to handle things together. If the other side won't listen to your requests, maybe that person is somebody to declutter...?

I know that sounds harsh, but people who always make you feel bad don't deserve to spend time with you!

I know...if that's your mom, your dad, or—even worse—your wife, you've got some work to do. Setting boundaries with your parents is not easy, but you can do it! If you don't feel good about being together with your wife, I want to encourage you to ask yourself, "Do I still love her? Do I still respect her? Can I think of our wedding day, where everything was so great? Do I want to figure things out with her, together? Is she willing to figure this relationship out?"

If yes, GO for it! Seek help! Go to a counselor, talk everything through with a good friend who can help you two to focus and not fight. And if that doesn't work, well, sometimes it's just not the right person.

No, I don't want to encourage you to break up with your lady. What I want is for you to have a really great, fulfilling, easy-going relationship where you feel seen, heard, respected, and supported. And I'm very, very, very sure that this is what your wife or girlfriend wants from you, too. The problem is that we often expect the other person to take care of our happiness. That's the wrong idea. You have to take care of your own happiness, your own good feelings (by now, you can handle these kinds of words!), your mood, your wellness, your energy. That way, your woman is free from the duty to make you happy. And yes, this applies to her too. Imagine how AWESOME that would feel. You tell each other what you need, what you expect, what you would love to experience, and you do it together. No guessing. Just clear and normal talking. No bitching around or yelling. Just doing kind, fun, and supportive things for each other. You can, because you took care of yourself first. You have the energy and the freedom to be nice to her. You don't expect her to make you happy, because you are already happy.

"God, Ronja, you are such a stupid...." (hey, did you call me bitch?). Well, if you are a pussy and can't deal with this, I can't help you. But you can help yourself! You can find out what you LOVE to do, what makes you happy, what you need to feel fit, healthy, energized, and creative. What do you want to do in your free time? What do you want to do for a living? How do you want to show up on the stage of life? You don't need anybody else but YOURSELF to change your world. And I'm sure if you can remember the love and happiness you felt on your wedding day, you can fix your relationship— because you will fix yourself, first. Talk with your lady. She has the same kinds of fears and challenges. Remember—if you just yell and fight with each other, nothing is going to change.

"What are you talking about? I have a brilliant relationship already. Don't talk to me in this way."

Hey man, I'm sorry! But I'm sure you have a friend who has the kind of relationship described above, yes? Tell him what I told you, and his world will change! Even better, give him this book after you're done reading it.

And hey, you'll have a journaling-buddy! Is there no way you'll tell anybody about this journaling thing? No worries, nobody will find out! I can keep a secret.

So. With each category of self-care, it breaks down to: WHAT is it that you want? Get really clear about this. Meet your future self, who is living this plan day-by-day and who achieved everything that you dream of. Get his advice. Get his support. And then, step by step, change yourself into the best future version of yourself you can imagine. Wow...how does that sound?

I'm so freaking proud that you are still reading and still following and still playing with me and still figuring out that this is a BIG FAT DEAL. The deal of YOUR LIFE! You can decide whatever you want, and this is...yes, I'll tell you again: SO powerful!

So, let's jump into the next chapter. Let's make things happen. You know what you want, you thought things through. Now we need ACTION!

Hey, you've come so far! All the plans and the big vision, you've done all the decluttering, inside and outside, and you're aware that taking good care of yourself is a really healthy thing to do. The things you do for yourself every day or every week, THEY sum up! They begin to change you step by step. Let's jump into HABITS!

6

"JUST FOLLOW YOUR JOY. ALWAYS. I THINK
THAT IF YOU DO THAT, LIFE WILL TAKE YOU ON
THE COURSE THAT IT'S MEANT TO TAKE YOU"

JONATHAN GROFF

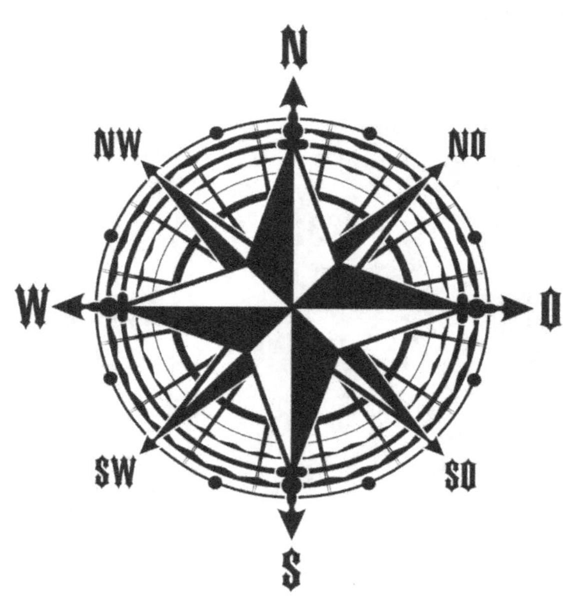

CHAPTER SIX

HABITS

HABITS ARE THE KEY

When I was about ten, my father (remember, the one with the messy office) had extreme lower back pain. He wasn't able to move for three days without having enormous pain. I still see him suffering, and at the time, I was thinking, "Oh no, my strong daddy is so weak." A physiotherapist came to our house every day to train with him, and she gave my father a lecture on the importance of fitness. It was his own fault. She then gave him exercises for his back to do daily. And he did. Every single freaking morning, he still does these exercises—plus five minutes on the home trainer at full speed. Takes him about fifteen minutes, plus a shower afterwards. He's eighty-one years old now, fit as a fiddle and looking good. Every year before New Year's Eve, he walks for more than two hours to our mountain cabin with a backpack. Step by step, without a hurry. He's up there first because the rest of us are busy taking care of the kids who need breaks to drink tea or rest, or someone has to pee. He just walks and arrives, totally in Zen mode.

Would he be so fit if he didn't invest these fifteen minutes for his daily workout? Nope!
Are fifteen minutes per day an exhausting amount of time to invest in your health and fitness? Nope!

It's an easy thing to define good little habits for yourself to do daily, weekly, or monthly. The hard thing is to stick with them. My father has been doing these exercises for thirty-three years now. That's over 12,000 times! Crazy right? But the result is just too cool!

So, how about asking your future self? "Not AGAIN?!" Hey, if this cool, healthy, fit, and radiant guy is not your role model (not my dad, YOUR future self), you are missing out!

I have another meditation for you, so you can really dive into your subconscious mind and get his answers. Is that too scary? Never mind trying something new. You don't have to, but you can...if you are brave enough to try. Tell me: WHY not? Huh? Why not meditate with me for fifteen minutes, and after that, you'll have the wisdom of your future self to implement right away? The cool thing about guided meditations is that you can experience the whole scene in full color and 4D, if you want. I can't promise that, but in my mastermind group, we do a guided meditation every week. It amazes me every time how clearly the situations appear to all the group members. They all hear the same text, and yet they each see totally different things. One guy is a hobby pilot, and his future self always meets him at the hangar because his future self flies more regularly and has a lot more experience, obviously. How cool is that? Other future-self meetings were on a mountaintop, in a café, ... you decide—or, way better, you'll just see where you meet, like in a movie.

Did I convince you to try this meditation? Yes? Go to www.joyismycompass.com/bookbonus.

You don't want to meditate? You dear wonderful stubborn idiot? No, I better talk nicely to you and treat you as kindly as I want you to treat me, right? But really: Doing it will blow your mind, because you'll have insights that you can't access without being in a meditative state of mind! It's easy. Just download it, put your earplugs in, sit on your sofa or a chair, and listen and do what I tell you. It's like story time. You listen to the story, and the pictures, the movie in your head will start automatically. DEAL?

Not doing it, no way? Well, get your journal out, young man, and write it out!

You can meet your future self wherever you want in your mind, then you can ask him: What do you do on a daily, weekly, or monthly basis? What kind of habits are non-negotiable for you? How did you get into such good shape, and how do you maintain it? It's all about habits, like my father's. If the ideas don't pop in your head easily, DO THE MEDITATION—or ask yourself: Well, he's in such great shape, he must do some kind of sport. Which kind? Hmmm, what do I like to do? What sport did I always want to try? You did this work already in the previous chapters, but now it's GAME TIME! You decide when, where, and what (and with whom). You decide on the new habits you want to install.

> My daddy: I've been doing my workout in the exact same order every day for 35 years now, right after waking up, I go to the living room on the white carpet (no mat required), then I go to the bedroom and sit on the home trainer (a very old version...but hey, you don't need the newest equipment), and do a little bicycle race for 5 minutes. After that, I take a shower, and then I read the newspaper in the kitchen.

That's an old man's habit if you think? Yeah, you don't have to do it my father's way. You have to do it YOUR way! This was only an example of how very specific you should decide on your habits. Your coach? Yes: Your future self.

Is that too lame? Not enough of a challenge? Well... I think it's nice to just start and build from there. I'm super bad at habits like doing sports, but I definitely feel better when I stick to it. When I talk myself out of doing yoga or a workout in the morning, I have back pain or headaches and tension in my neck and shoulders. My body is telling me to just DO the workout and take care of myself. But hey, I'm not perfect, and I'm hanging in here together with you. Let's get our shit together, okay?

It's not only sports habits, but those are the hardest for me. Other habits I also want to integrate daily are:

- Journaling - at least 750 words per day (Check out 750words.com!)

- Meditate - at least fifteen minutes of going deep and getting all the cool answers for the day, new ideas, and support from within (yes, my future self is a regular guest at this meeting)

- EFT - Emotional Freedom Technique (Meet my guy, Brad Yates, on YouTube. He's the best and has a video for any topic of your life. WTF is EFT? Just try it. It's free and weird, and you better make sure that your neighbors don't see you doing this! My husband, Ken, makes fun of me big-time when I'm tapping. But guess what? I don't care. This technique is life-changing in getting rid of old limiting beliefs, fears, and other worries you never ever told anybody about. Go and try it...but if you try anything new and weird, DO MY MEDITATION FIRST!

I love you...do you know that? I love you for being here, for reading this, for sticking to this witchy lady from Switzerland with her Japanese husband and all her overwhelmingly weird suggestions. You are the coolest guy for reading this book!

Write down all the habits you want to attain. Write them ALL down! You have no idea what kind of habits shaped your future self? Well, you can go get my list then? No? Okay, so you write your own list then? Still no idea?

Have you heard of Andy Frisella? A friend of mine told me recently about all the habits Andy Frisella's 75 Hard Challenge demands.

I listened to the podcast, where Andy explains the details himself. He says "fuck" in every single sentence, which sounds so funny to me, as a Swiss country girl. I imagined the censorship bleep sound from American T.V. the whole time. But that's not the point, and luckily, there are no bleeps in a podcast.

I can tell you that I'm the softy here when demanding nice new habits for you. Andy is a hardcore machine, and he's not kidding around. His challenge goes like this:

I quote Andy:

1. Follow a fucking diet: Whatever fucking goal you have, e.g., losing body fat. No fucking junk food, no alcohol, no sweets, no nibbling chips. Zero deviation, and no fucking cheating.
2. Work out twice a day for at least forty-five minutes. Whatever workout. One workout is inside, one workout is outdoors. If it's cold or hot or a tornado, you're still gonna fucking do it. It has to get done.
3. Drink a gallon of water every day. This is gonna teach you discipline. It's healthy. And don't fucking think this is easy. The simple things are sometimes the most difficult.
4. Read ten pages of a self-development book where you can learn something. An actual book. This will benefit you greatly.
5. Make a progress picture every day.

He says, "This will cultivate extreme discipline, and you'll learn to say no. If you are weak and you can't say no to alcohol if your friends are around, just fucking don't go to this birthday party then."

The BIG point is: You have to finish seventy-five days in a row. If you fuck it up, you have to start over. Eat a handful of candy and you have to start all over again.

Andy, if you ever read my book, thank you for this. It makes my demands of my readers look so easy!

Maybe your future self is a fan of Andy Frisella, and he's been following the 75 Hard Challenge for years? Maybe you will be listening to all his episodes starting today? There are so many cool role models out there, and you can become one too! First for your friends, for your lady, for your kids, for your people. By just doing it YOUR way!

I don't like too many rules. I like it when I GET TO CHOOSE what I want to do. And I can choose. I choose my own rules for my habits, but I'm super inspired by this kind of commitment of the 75 Hard Challenge. You can choose, too. This is cool, right?

Bo Eason is another great man to follow and learn from. He teaches in his book that there is no Plan B for your A-game. His is the 66-Day Challenge. He says that after sixty-six days of sticking to your new habit, it'll be easier for you to DO your habit than it would be to NOT do it.

You see all these numbers of days. Some say it takes twenty-one days, or thirty days to install a new habit...whatever goal you are setting for yourself, whatever challenge you're committing yourself to, START! And then just DO it, every single day! Will you fail? Of course! Is that super bad? Not at all. Just get back into the game the next day. And if you're doing the 75 Hard Challenge, you're back to square one.

I like to use trackers. In the Joy Academy, we always use trackers. Either you use one of the various templates on the book-bonus page (www.joyismycompass.com/bookbonus), or you design your own. One of the wonder women in my mastermind drew all the tasks on a whiteboard. This board now stares at her in her bathroom, waiting to get colored in.

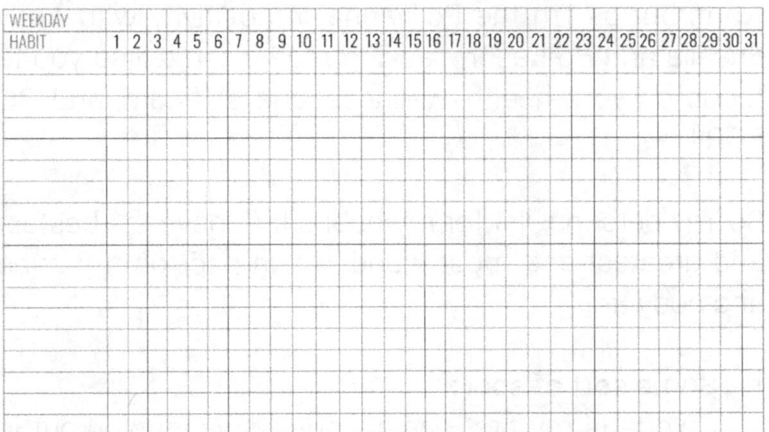

"Yeah, nice, but WHAT shall I commit to?"

Ask your future self! What does he do?

I bet he does some sporty activities? Break them down in detail like:

1. **Thirty pushups**
2. **Two-minute plank**
3. **One hundred squats**

Or you just write down: Workout for forty-five minutes. Drink more water? Drink a gallon? Drink two liters? Drink less soda? If you drink five big bottles of soda every day, you could challenge yourself and go for only two? Guess what: YOU choose. I know, it's annoying to choose so freaking fucking much...just kidding. I love to choose! I want you to feel this freedom. You can choose! You can drink whatever you want all day long. Vodka, gin and tonic, beer. You can do drugs and use other feeling-suppressing substances. You can do whatever you want, but as I'm the Pollyanna of positivity with Andy Frisella and Bo Eason backing me up, I'm telling you to focus on your health, wellness, and self-care, and GO FOR IT!

So, my personal list for my habits that have the bestest and greatest and most wonderful impact on my mind and body are:

- **Some sort of sport**
  Yoga is my first choice, but a sweaty workout in the morning in my living room is a good way to start the day and then shower (I like to earn my shower).
- **Drink lots of water or herbal tea**
- **Eat yummy AND healthy**
  My food is so good. I chose to go vegan when I heard the screaming cows as I was passing the slaughterhouse in Zurich. That was the point when I finally decided to go all in.

- **Journaling**

  Just free flow or affirmations or a good old Be-Do-Have list, or an ideal day, or just some words...

- **Meditate**

  Mostly I do a freestyle guided meditation in my head. I recorded so many that I just go and see what comes up... (I have some up my sleeve for you to use and choose for free at www.joyismycompass.com/bookbonus)

- **Reading/Learning**

  Before bed or during the day. I love online courses in all the possible topics, and I love audiobooks.

- **EFT**

  That's one of my favorites, as I told you, check out Brad Yates on YouTube.

- **No phone in the bedroom**

  I regularly cheat on this one... stupid me... I'm a social media addict, and I should know better and just leave my device in the living room.

- **7-8 hours of sleep**

  When that's not possible, I often take a nap in the afternoon, like a grandma. I love my power naps of thirty-three minutes.

- **Gratitude practice before falling asleep**

  I don't journal on what I'm grateful for that day, but this would be super powerful, too! I just go through the day in my thoughts and say thank you for all the good and cool things that happened.

The ones I REALLY have to put some effort into daily are: Sport, meditating, journaling, EFT, no phone in the bedroom, sleep. The ones which are totally installed, non-negotiable, and as normal as brushing my teeth are food, water, reading, and gratitude.

So, now it's your turn! How hard do you want to challenge yourself? Do you want to go for 75 Hard? What do you want to change?

- Say "no," when you mean "no"?
- Stop watching T.V. for four hours a day?
- Get fit enough to hike up a certain mountain?
- Be kind to your lady every day?
- Stop yelling at your kids every morning? (What do you need to actually do this? More time? Okay, you can get up earlier—oh, and exercise in the morning for your own energy. If you take care of yourself first, caring for others is so much easier!)
- Stop moaning all day long?
- Be present in conversations?
- No phone at the dinner table?
- Eat your food with full presence and no distraction, like T.V. or phone?
- Go and play basketball in the neighborhood after work?
- Run five miles a day?

Nope, I'm not telling you what to do. YOU decide! And you really have to want to do it. Otherwise, it's for the birds. Whatever habit you want to start with from scratch, it will be hard. It sucks. But the rewards will be so damn good!

Talk to your future self in your head. See him teasing you that you won't do it, you lazy dude...hear his voice and see his annoyingly fit and healthy and strong body. See his smile and feel his contagious energy. Can you convince yourself that becoming HIM is possible?

So just begin. You don't have to start with the perfect set of habits. Just start and adjust while you go. Print out that tracker, fill in the habits. Any day you do it (daily, of course, right?), color in the according square. That's all.

What helps to stick to it:
Get an accountability partner.
Celebrate every week that you're still doing it.
Enjoy coloring in the fields like a proud little boy.
Have your future self in your mind. He's rooting for ya!

If you want to know more about managing habits and why they are so super powerful, I recommend the book: *Atomic Habits* by James Clear. This is such an amazing book in which he introduces the idea of "habit stacking" and how you should make your bad habits really annoyingly difficult. For example, put your T.V. in a closet, or always take the batteries out of your remote and hide them in some ridiculous spot. That way, if you want to watch T.V., a lot of effort is needed to get there.

On the other hand, make your good habits really easy. Only buy healthy ingredients, and no chips or candy. Put your kettlebell and sports mat out in front of your bed so that you are reminded immediately after you get up. There's some really good advice in his book! If you don't like reading, get an app where you can listen to audiobooks. I love Audible and Scribd. Check them out!

Hey, and now HAVE FUN! You're doing this for YOU! You'll feel better, full of energy, gain strength, you'll sleep better, your mood will be elevated...the struggle of beginning to change is so worth it! You're your man!

If you want to use the progress-picture habit, go and do it daily...or weekly. You'll notice the difference, and that's super rewarding and motivating!

I can't wait to hear all your wins and aha-moments you've had because you are just a superhero. And your superhero future self is helping you improve every day, while you enjoy that your heart is beating, you are ALIVE, and you have choices!

7

> "YOU DECIDE WHAT BRINGS YOU JOY. DO MORE OF THAT. LIFE IS SUPPOSED TO BE FUN!"
>
> RONJA SAKATA

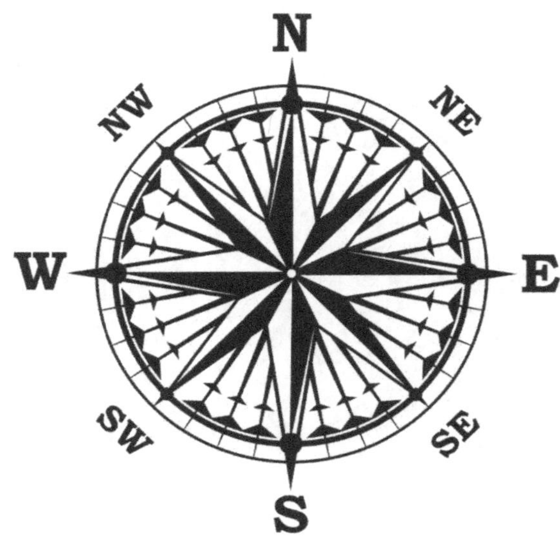

CHAPTER SEVEN

CREATE JOY

YOU ROCK!

Hey man, we've made it to the last chapter! You are just a hero to me! You thought through your big fat vision, decluttered your home like a mad man, decluttered your beliefs and old wounds, decided what your self-care should look like, and put into practice daily, weekly, or monthly habits. HOW COOL IS THAT?

Now let's throw some icing on this cake. Fun treats that will put a big grin on your face. This is as personal as all the other things we've discussed! What's fun for you doesn't have to be fun for your wife, girlfriend, or future girlfriend, but guess what—you're again focusing on YOU, and you'll have the most benefit out of this.

- What brings you joy?
- A clean, shiny car?
- Dashing down a powdery mountain on your snowboard?
- Watching football?
- Singing country songs around a campfire with your guitar in your lap?
- Going for a walk with your dog?
- Your bulletproof coffee?
- New sneakers for parkour jumps?
- A beer with your gang?
- Dancing in a club?

See...the examples couldn't be more different. That's why you have to write this list on your own. Write down one hundred things that bring you joy.
You're thinking, "One hundred? Are you insane?"
You know by now that I'm a crazy woman, so just do it. Ten is too easy. Twenty is easy too...but one hundred? That's when you really have to think of all the BIG and little things that bring a smile to your face!

Go for it! One hundred things. NOW!

1.

2.

3.

4.

5.

6.

7.

8.

9.

10.

11.

12.

13.

14.

15.

16.

17.

18.

CREATE JOY

19.

20.

21.

22.

23.

24.

25.

26.

27.

28.

29.

30.

31.

32.

33.

34.

35.

36.

37.

38.

39.

40.

41.

42.

43.

44.

45.

46.

47.

48.

49.

50.

51.

52.

53.

54.

55.

56.

57.

58.

59.

60.

61.

62.

63.

64.

65.

66.

67.

68.

69.

70.

71.

72.

73.

74.

75.

76.

77.

78.

CREATE JOY

79.

80.

81.

82.

83.

84.

85.

86.

87.

88.

89.

90.

91.

92.

93.

94.

95.

96.

97.

98.

99.

100.

This is your to-do list for every day. Do as many things on this list as possible. I always say to do at least three, because you are worth the effort, right? More joy brings more fun. A fun and joyful person is cooler to be around. With good energy around you, you'll attract success, the greatest friends, and the nicest lady. You'll be more relaxed, and since you take the best care of yourself you have no expectations for your surroundings that they take care of you. You are FREE! So damn free! You don't have to please anyone but yourself. You did your sport in the morning already. You enjoy your bulletproof coffee at home as much as you do a weekend of heli-skiing. You feel good. You choose to feel good.

Is that still too much for you to read? Do you feel uncomfortable? You don't want to be the good-mood man in your team, in your family, in your neighborhood? You choose. AGAIN, you choose who you want to be. You can enjoy your good feelings because you take such good care of yourself and have all these amazing habits, quietly and "secretly"...but I tell you, it'll shine through. People will recognize the difference, and you'll become a role model for many around you, without even knowing it.

So now, as you are in such a good mood and state, let's do some fun stuff for others. I can tell you that your lady will be THRILLED if you go all-in to bringing fun and joy into her life, too. She knows that she's responsible for her own joy and wellbeing, but your actions are like extra treats in the day. These things work for kids, grandparents, roommates, whoever you live with. It even works for yourself!

Some of the things on this list may be perceived as super romantic... you can give them any title you want, and of course, you know your lady (and family) the best... just try and earn the smiles and happy faces:

- Write/draw little nice or fun sticky notes and place them into lunchboxes, in the fridge, at the door, in the purse.
- Buy a favorite drink/treat/fruit/juice and hide it somewhere with a little treasure hunt. Arrows are always so, so cool...for kids AND grownups!
- Buy flowers. Just because. Maybe you'll have it

delivered with a card? I never get flowers from my husband. In the seventeen years I've been living with him in Zurich, I once got gorgeous roses—but he got them for free at work! Well, I buy my own flowers now, but I would love to get some for sure! This always works! But, if your girl/lady/wife is freaking out and asking whether you're hiding something because you cheated on her or something stupid like this, sit her down and give her this book. This stupid behavior of our society crushes the fun and joy! How can these flowers be a sign of something bad? She needs a reframe. Stay calm and nice and set her straight in a friendly way. If she can't enjoy flowers just because you are the greatest guy to be with...well, she'll miss out on flowers in the future.

- Smuggle a little gift in her handbag, or school bag, or briefcase (you see, I just don't know with whom you are living). Like a box in a box in a box in a box and inside, there is a little chocolate? Or again, a message? If you are not the message-writing guy, be assured that you can write "I love you," everyday, always and forever. This never gets old!

- What I also love is not so romantic, but even better—do the laundry, do the grocery shopping, do whatever chore is actually her chore or the kids', your roommate's, or Grandma's chores! It's just so nice if you come home and hear, "Oh, that's already done!" I highly recommend you have a deal at your home about who works on what, which things are just THIS person's job and how you organize the whole cooking-dirty-dishes-never-ending cycle. If you live alone at the moment, you can learn for your future, if you want to share an apartment. So, when everybody has their jobs, it's possible to do this job for them and surprise them. You already heard that my husband is the laundry-boss in our house. If I'm working at home and I'm REALLY nice, I sometimes wash a machine full of laundry and hang it up. When the sun is shining, and the laundry hangs in the sunshine, I get extra points! My job is to wake up our girl every morning and bring her to bed nearly every night. So, if he does that for me, I thank him so much and really enjoy this favor. Do you get what I mean? If she's not happy with the way you did it, have a serious conversation with your lady again. If YOU are the perfectionist in the house, CHILL! We all have to take life less seriously and enjoy ourselves, our company, and the kindness of others. If you do the dishes for me, I'll be forever grateful and thank you one thousand times! Just so you know!

- Any other ideas to surprise your family, your lady, your roommates? Maybe a prank is funny? I'm not at all the prank-girl, and I get super upset if things break or other bad things happen just because of a prank. ("Hey, you just said to CHILL and take life less seriously." I know. I hate pranks… I still have to learn to stay cool when it comes to pranks!) My husband always creeps into our apartment and appears with bulging eyes at our kitchen door window. I ALWAYS jump because I'm so scared. Mika, our daughter, learned quickly. The many times she's scared me… I can't count them. Well, I can handle that. But like, drowned laptops with broken hard discs or things like that? Don't do that! Sorry to be a party pooper, but you know what? You can do whatever YOU want…once!

So, now you are the kindest, most caring man, who buys flowers, writes notes and brings fun into his home. Doesn't that sound appealing at all? Just try it. Try new things. Try it for a week or longer—don't give up at the first attempt of creating joy at home, if things don't change immediately. If your relationship has been difficult recently, it may require lots of patience until your attempts begin to soften your lady. Just do it, and I promise you, change will happen. And if you have the best relationships under your roof already, your home will thrive even more. That's what I love about all these little things: They make the world (our home) a better place wherever your starting point is!

RANDOM ACTS OF KINDNESS

Now let's take it to the streets. Do you know the term, "Random acts of kindness?" I love it, and again it's a creative playground to bring more fun, light, happiness, and a good mood into your neighborhood, your village, city, or country. And with social media, you can influence even more people by showing off what your idea is. So, people around the globe can steal that idea from you and do it in their own neighborhood. This ripple effect makes me happy by just writing about it.

The most important thing is that YOU have fun doing these random acts of kindness. Do what suits you, ok? If you have a smile on your face while preparing the action, you win twice or even more.

I have loads of ideas, little and big ones. Not all of them will be possible to do where you live, but they shall inspire your own creativity and your unique kind of fun and kindness.

Buy a package of sidewalk chalk and go write or draw cool stuff onto the street!

"Are you crazy, Ronja Sakata? This makes me look super silly and childish!"
Do you really care that much about what other people think of you? Screw them. You are bringing fun to the streets.
"No, I can't draw, and I won't write anything."
Hey, no problem bro! Just do what you LIKE to do. We are told way too much what to do, but sidewalk chalk drawings are voluntary, for sure!

If you are an artistic guy, or you just like the thought of writing a compliment, a wish, or even an inspirational quote on the ground, like, "You are beautiful, inside and out!" ("Oh, no, come on, you cheesy woman!") "I wish you a wonderful day!" ("Lame, but okay…") "You rock!" ("Better?") "Go for it!" ("Okay…") "Don't let fear stand in the way of your dreams!" ("Okay, lady, you're getting closer here!") "Impossible is nothing!" (Adidas will send you a check for that…) You get what I mean…just play around like a kid!

Draw a hopscotch on the sidewalk and place a stone there so that everyone passing by can hop for fun. There are videos on Facebook of random people, grownups of all age groups, hopping through with a big smile, caught on film with a hidden camera. Maybe you can install a hidden camera too? Or hide behind the bushes? No, if that's too weird, don't do it! Just enjoy that you brought happiness into these people's lives with the effort of three minutes and some chalk. That's so worth it, right?

What's very cool and easy with sidewalk chalk, too, is a treasure hunt. With arrows and signs and maybe little letters, you can create a whole circuit for anybody who is in for some fun. This can be a really big thing in your neighborhood. Imagine how everybody would want to go on your treasure-hunt-circuit-tour! And the video will go viral, and Ellen will invite you to her show. How about that? You don't want that AT ALL? No problem. Just don't share it on social media, AND you'll have to tell your fans it's a secret. But please, if you do something cool because you were inspired by this book and you're proud of it, would you be so kind as to send me a picture or a video? hello@ronjasakata.com Thank you!

So far, there's the idea of a chalk-game. What about little notes? A year ago, I had this idea of the Joy-Ripple-Effect, and I created joy-cards, where you have templates with nice messages or plain ones for your own personalized messages. On the next two pages, there are joy-cards for you to cut out or copy. Pin them and stick them everywhere you go. In public transportation, underneath windshield wipers, in a shopping cart, on a can of pineapples... put the joy cards wherever you want! Let your message put a smile on the finder's face. The link on the card leads to a free Joy Challenge with lots of little inspirations on how we can pay the joy forward and put momentum on the Joy-Ripple-Effect. I know, I know, I overuse the word JOY, but I deeply believe that we need more joy on our planet and it starts with YOU, yourselves, and your homes (you did a freaking great job with all that decluttering and creating good vibes...you are my hero!). And then our neighborhoods and our cities and our countries... I literally see the waves of the ripples flowing outwards, like on a lake. This is a real thing. You are kind to YOURSELF first, to others second, and these people pass it on. YOU have an insanely big impact on the planet. Yes, you alone. The power of one kind word, the magic of one random act of kindness. Thank you for changing the world, man. Thank you!

Cut the next page out and tape the cards to lamp posts and park benches, where you live! If you don't want to ruin this book or the page is missing already, you'll find the templates on the book-bonus page:

www.joyismycompass.com/bookbonus

YOU ROCK!
ENJOY YOUR DAY.
MAKE IT A GOOD
ONE, FOR YOU!

GO YOU!
YOU'VE GOT
THIS! YES, YOU!

HEY SUPERSTAR!
DO SOMETHING YOU
LIKE TODAY. BRING
FUN INTO YOUR DAY!

THIS MESSAGE
IS HERE TO TELL
YOU, THAT EVERY-
THING WILL WORK
OUT JUST FINE!

THIS IS YOUR LIFE!
WHY WOULD YOU DO
THINGS YOU HATE?
WHAT COULD YOU
CHANGE TODAY?

THE GOOD NEWS:
YOU CAN ONLY
CHANGE YOURSELF.
SO FOCUS ON
YOUR IMPROVE-
MENTS ONLY!

YOU ARE DOING
GREAT! JUST
KEEP EVOLVING
& GROWING!
YOU'VE GOT THIS!

MAKE YOURSELF
NUMBER "1" IN
YOUR LIFE, THEN
SERVE OTHERS FULL
OF ENERGY!

Write your own messages on the next page!
Or download the template on the book-bonus page:

www.joyismycompass.com/bookbonus

Way to go! And thank you for spreading kind messages!

If you are in for putting some money in the game, that's great fun, too! Write a message (joy card or not) that reads, "Hey man, this is for you. Buy something nice," and attach one or five or ten or twenty or fifty dollars to the note...wow, imagine the expression on the person's face who finds this blessing. Wrap it around a tree, on a park bench...wherever. A letter with money.

But it doesn't have to be a secret and a surprise. Just starting a genuine conversation with a homeless person, asking about his or her day, can be a blessing, too. Listening and being present—that's a big thing in today's world. Not only with a homeless person, with anybody you meet. What's also very cool is to give compliments often. To complete strangers! It's so freaking interesting how they'll be received.

> **"A compliment? From a guy I don't know?**
> **What's his intention?"**

If you just walk ahead, she or he will maybe stay stuck in their tracks for a moment, but after that, for sure, they will smile and take it all in! A compliment is like a huge gift! But only compliment if you really feel that way. Fake compliments stink! Think about how you receive compliments. Do you say: "Thank you very much!" or "That's so kind, thank you!" or do you dismiss it with an immediate compliment back or by playing it down? This is SO interesting! It depends a lot on how you learned this as a kid. Being confident and proud of ourselves is something we can relearn if it was a no-go as a kid. Give compliments often, and try to receive them with a simple thank you. That's so good!

And the last thing: Have fun, wherever, whenever possible. If there is a slide, go slide. If there is a swing, go swing. If you can bring fun into a meeting, a dinner gathering, a personal conversation, create joy for yourself and the others. Remember the one hundred things-that-bring-you-joy list? This list is GOLDEN, and you can write more things on the list every day. This list is the library of creating joy for yourself and the people around you in all seasons and in all situations.

How about having a nice chat with your hot future self again? What is he doing to create joy all day long? He's freaking good at this joy game. He's so popular in his job, at home, in his neighborhood. Not in the showing-off sense of popular. He just makes everybody feel so good when they spend time with him. He sees people. He's present. He listens. He is such a nice guy. No, not a weak guy. A really cool, genuine guy who is so fucking inspiring to everyone around him. He chose himself. Everybody can tell that. He's just himself. He doesn't give a fuck about what people around him say or think about him. He's doing his thing, and his thing is to enjoy this fabulous life. To create every day as ideally as he can. He grows with his habits. He takes care of his body and his soul. He's confident, not conceited at all. He has his fears and his doubts, but he walks through them with a trusting feeling that he'll be okay. He is such a great guy, living his life without regrets, making memories with the people he loves, bringing fun and joy to everyone who spends time with him.

This is you! You just have a journey in front of you to become this guy! You have complete power over this transformation, and only you know how far away you are from this annoying superman who shows off how he has all his shit together! Don't be jealous. Enjoy the journey.

I remember there is a YouTube-video—which I can't find anymore, but anyway—the message was: You don't go to a cinema and only watch the happy end. You want to see the whole story. You don't go to a concert only to listen to the last song. You want to listen to the whole concert. If you go river rafting, you want to enjoy the whole ride, not only the last bit. Enjoy your journey, but be aware that not one day is guaranteed. For me, it's a mix between self-care and pushing myself forward, a balance between chasing my goals and just enjoying the moment and chilling out. This is the art of living life, in and out of our comfort zones, by holding our own standards high and focusing on creating JOY.

Your JOY compass is now set. You are so good to go and do this. Every day you go out there and ROCK your life. Change takes time, but go all-in. I'm so proud of you that you read this book. This takes guts. This takes balls!

(Am I even allowed to say that?) Thank you for spending time with me! Thank you for being YOU! I love you man, right now, and I'm secretly even more in love with your future self! I'm cheering you on, and if our paths ever cross, I'll congratulate you personally for creating your glorious life, day by day! Take good care of yourself, and enjoy every heartbeat!

LET'S CHOP THIS WOOD!
BOOK BONUSES WAIT FOR YOU HERE:
www.joyismycompass.com/bookbonus
Your Future Self and I are celebrating you and all the steps you took already, you rockstar! Thank you for being you and for keeping up the good work, one log at a time!

CAN YOU HELP?

Thank You for Reading My Book!

I really appreciate all of your feedback, and I love hearing what you have to say. I need your input to make the next version of this book and my future books better.

Please leave me an honest review on Amazon letting me know what you thought of the book.

Thanks so much!

Ronja ♡

PEOPLE THAT HAVE INSPIRED ME

- Brendon Burchard

  He wrote so many books, and you have to read them all! ;) *High Performance Habits* and *Life's Golden Ticket* are my most favorite for sure! Thanks to Brendon's live event Experts Academy I met the most amazing people, and I got to see Bo Eason live.

- Bo Eason

  I love Bo Eason, the author of *There Is No Plan B for Your A-Game*. He's on YouTube with his mind-blowing storytelling power. I'll put the links to my favorite videos of Bo on the book-bonus page, ok? I met Bo in California at his live event, and I can highly recommend getting near this powerhouse. His energy is contagious and his expertise just brilliant.

- Jesse Itzler

  Living with a SEAL and *Living with the Monks* - these two books, you must listen to. Jesse is the guy who invented "The Happiness Meter," and I told you about his TED Talk in my book. I'm in Jesse's program called BYLR (Build Your Life Resume), and I again met the coolest and most wonderful guys and girls.

- Sara Blakley

  She became the world's youngest female self-made billionaire in 2012. Jesse Itzler is her husband, and I admire how these two totally different, super inspiring people create their life together full of adventure, fun and with a free spirit! Follow both of them on social media and get inspired!

- Leonie Dawson

  She taught me about not settling down in Stuckville, just travel through! Best analogy ever for being an entrepreneur.

- Adriene Michler

  This lady is my personal trainer in my living room at 4:44 or later in the day. If you want to try Yoga in secret, this is my recommendation: Yoga with Adriene. But there are loads of guys out there too. Check them out, yoga is cool!

- Andy Frisella

  I hope so much that you are intrigued by the 75 Hard Challenge, and that you let Andy have an impact on your attitude and mindset. More in your face than with Andy, I don't know where you could get that. Thanks to Mister Frisella, my habits-chapter looks so easy. Listen to Andy on all the challenges and get inspired daily!

REFERENCES

These books had a big impact on my mindset and how I do life, so I can highly recommend them to you!

- Bronnie Ware, **The Top Five Regrets of the Dying**, Hay House Inc., 2019

  I started the book with these, do you remember? The book is very eye-opening to all the things we could do NOW, when we're here and not when we're about to die.

- James Clear, **Atomic Habits**, Avery, 2018

  This is a MUST read. Really. Mandatory. No joke. Read this book next.

- Jens Corssen, **The Way of the Self-Developer**, Pronoun, 2016

  This book honestly changed my life. I listened to it on repeat, and I could tell you all of his stories and insights for eight hours straight. Read it too!

- Marie Kondo, **The Life-Changing Magic of Tidying Up**, Ten Speed Press, 2014

  If you read this book or watch videos of her work online, your decluttering game will get stronger for sure!

The Joy Compass

THIS IS YOUR LIFE!
WHY ON EARTH WOULD
YOU WASTE YOUR TIME WITH
THINGS AND PEOPLE YOU DON'T
LIKE. FIND OUT WHAT YOU WANT
AND CREATE A LIFE FULL OF
FUN AND JOY AND THINGS YOU
LOVE TO DO, SPENDING TIME
WITH PEOPLE YOU ADORE!

Hey lady wonderful, are you ready to dive into this book? I am together with you and I want you to know: I see you – I hear you – I adore you.

You want to change things up in your life and you know what? You've got this! You are powerful and magical. You have the wisdom of the whole Universe inside of you.

You deserve to
» play BIG
» take up space
» say what you WANT
» GET what you want
» create JOY for yourself
» set boundaries and say NO
» say YES whole heartedly
» be YOU every single day
» change who you want to be any time of the day, because you grow and change and evolve with every new connection, with every interaction, with every lesson learned, with every decision made.

Thank you for investing in your growth. Your future you will thank you so much for the effort you are putting in today. Let's start, shall we?

Ronja ♡

CONTENTS

MY OWN STORY

The Fuel to My Joy

When I was sixteen, I glued little empty boxes on a giant piece of cardboard, cut little doors into every box, and drew numbers on them. I created an advent calendar for my boyfriend. My friend Silvia sighed, "I would have to grab me a really nice boyfriend if I ever want to get a present like this!"

Like any good friend, I kept that in mind.

A year later, she dated the coolest guy. He was a fellow leader in our scout-division. In November 1994, I called him. "Do you have an idea yet, for a Christmas present for your lady?"

"Nope!"

So, I told him the story about last year, and he loved the idea. I brought him some empty boxes to create the calendar. Silvia was so delighted—she loved opening the presents day by day.

On the tenth of December, he was killed in an avalanche in the Swiss mountains. It was devastating. Fourteen little thoughtful presents and fourteen heartfelt letters were left of the love in the grave. This was the most beautiful and most heartbreaking thing ever.

Standing at his open grave, something clicked, hard, in my heart and soul: This life-game is not forever. You have no guarantee for any day or year. Any moment could be your last. That's hard to learn at seventeen, but it doesn't really depend on your age. The first time you become really, totally aware of this fact... it's a punch in the face.

Eleven years followed with too many funerals for friends my age. A motorcycle accident, another avalanche, a suicide, then the best friend of my sister died. Anja was twenty-five when she dropped dead of a heart attack. Oh wow... no dangerous sport involved, no risky ski-tour, no overlooked speed limit. She was at home, and her boyfriend, a med-school student, did all he could to bring her back... she was gone.

THIS was when I decided to not only just appreciate life, but to refuse to live a second longer by any compromises. From this day on, I declared to myself, I'll live my life on my own terms.

Today, I no longer do things I don't like. I don't do things only to please others. If I do anything or say anything or go anywhere, I do it because I WANT TO! I could be dead tomorrow, so TODAY I live life to the fullest. I enjoy my day! I'm as kind as I can be to everybody I meet. I spend time with people I love. I treasure the people I love. I go to places I want to see. I take care of my body. I'm ALL IN.

While I certainly got one, I don't believe we need a wakeup call like the death of a loved one or a near death experience ourselves. You are reading this book, and that's all you need right now—but don't get me wrong. You still have to do the work. You have to think about what YOU want in your life. You have to decide that this day, today, is your BEST day—and tomorrow will be even better!

Beyond showing you how to achieve this freedom, I will also tell you stories of my life, cheering you on all the way.

Thank you so much for your trust and your bravery to DO this! If you read this book, if you answer the questions, if you do the work, and if you think about what you want, it will change your life.

When I was thinking about writing this book, I had always envisioned a women's- and a men's version. I know in these days, this could be received as sexist. That's the last thing I want to achieve. I only want to address the fact that we women are more open to the "life-improving" stuff. For the guys, it quickly gets too airy-fairy... but I promise you, the "girl version" is not at all like that.

You'll find the male-version in the beginning of this book. It's the same book, but I'll be talking "their language" (I hope!) and sometimes share different stories than on this side. My goal is to encourage men to take better care of themselves, to be nice to themselves, and not be so hard on themselves. And to be nice and gentle with their lady, if they have one at their side. I know, that's a big challenge! But I like challenges, and I like men so much. We are all so different and unique, and that's awesome! This book speaks more to the feminine side, so continue if you're curious or switch to the "other book" if you are more into an "in-your-face" book.

Remember life can be short. Very short. It can be over this afternoon or go on for another fifty years! So, the goal of this book is to get you to enjoy every day of your life, while walking toward your big fat vision, taking exquisite care of yourself, and creating joy for all the people you meet every day, whether it be a family member or a stranger on the street.

Deal? Are you all in?

One last motivation that brings out the urgency of the work in this book even more:
Have you heard of the book, *The Top Five Regrets of the Dying*? Bronnie Ware is the author, and she has collected these top five regrets from uncountable conversations with dying patients during the years that she was working as a palliative care nurse.

They are:

1. I wish I'd had the courage to live a life true to myself, not the life others expected of me.
2. I wish I hadn't worked so hard.
3. I wish I'd had the courage to express my feelings.
4. I wish I had stayed in touch with my friends.
5. I wish that I had let myself be happier.

You can read the book, of course, for deeper inspiration, but thinking through these points yourself is even better.

1. I wish I'd had the courage to live a life true to myself, not the life others expected of me.

This is such a big point for us ladies. Of course, also men have to deal with the expectations of their parents or other relatives concerning their choices, but women want to make sure that everybody else is happy before we even consider investing some time or thought for ourselves. I say 'we,' because I was the same. Now, I can happily say that I only do what is true to myself. That's my check for ANYthing I do or say or create. Let's drop the others' expectations and think through *our* dreams and *our* personal vision for *our*selves. We can't please everyone around us, but creating a life which pleases YOU is beneficial for everyone around you. Imagine yourself super happy in your own designed life. That feels good, right? Your partner, your family, your neighbors, they will get inspired, OR they don't deserve you in their lives! End of story.

2. I wish I hadn't worked so hard.

Whatever you do for a living, whether you are in a corporate job, an entrepreneur, a stay-at-home mom, or a combination of all of these: Working too hard takes away time spent with your friends, time for yourself, time with your kids. Yep, also as a stay-at-home mom, you can work so hard that it feels like you had NO TIME with the kids on certain days. We'll work through this!

3. I wish I'd had the courage to express my feelings.

I never had any issues with expressing my feelings. I think I can't NOT express my feelings. I'm an open book. Even crying like crazy in the lecture hall with three hundred other students because the man I was in love with didn't want me to be his girlfriend... I don't care. That's why I can help you go all-in in this life department. It doesn't mean that you have to cry wherever you are! Not at all. It does mean that I'd like to encourage you to pay attention if tears or deep feelings come up somewhere "inconvenient", don't apologize, don't feel ashamed. You are just crying right now because something happened that made you cry. Expressing your feelings can also mean that you say what you think and don't tone down your expression out of fear of offending the other person. My wish is that after reading and working through this book, you will DECIDE how you want to show up in this life and stay truer than true to YOURSELF.

4. I wish I had stayed in touch with my friends.

Friends are pure gold—especially the ones you can count on at any time of the day, in any situation. The ones you can talk with for hours, and it feels like ten minutes. The ones who are here for you, whatever happens. I have friends from primary school days and others I've met only recently, and it feels like we've known each other for several lifetimes. Taking care of our friendships is one priority we'll work through in this book too.

5. I wish that I had let myself be happier.

How do you answer when someone asks, "How are you?" I have a ton of resources for you to invest in happiness and sustain it through your everyday life. Happiness is a choice and a mindset, and that's why it's so intertwined with our thoughts. Spirals of thought can lead us directly into the hell of overthinking everything. I want to show you lots of possibilities to ride the spiral *up,* into the heavens of ease and flow, happiness and good feelings, self-worth and self-esteem, independence and power.

Does this sound too good to be true? It actually can feel that way sometimes, but then I remind myself: You are in charge of your life, YOU design it, you create it, you are one hundred percent responsible for everything in your life. As soon as you own your mood, your thoughts, and your actions, you are free to be happy any time of the day.

"WHAT? I'm responsible for everything in my life? Give me a break! That's not true!"

I like it when you get upset and call me out! Let's dive into this book, and you can feel free to tell me afterwards if it was worth the work. I want to persuade you to do this for yourself. Not for me, for YOU!

We'll begin with your dream life. The life you don't even think you could have. To get what you want, you first have to KNOW what you want... so let's get started in the next chapter:

MY BIG FAT VISION

Everything Is possible

"What do you want?"

That's a question we are not so used to being asked, right? With all the expectations and the taking-what-I-can-get mentality, we dare not ask ourselves: "What do I want?"

When I pose this question to my coaching clients, some of them shrug, and some of them whisper things like: "I don't know! I mean, I have to go to work, right? I have to earn money...so why should it be important what I want?"

I'd like to switch things around here. First, we'll find out what you want, and *then* we'll figure out a way to get it, ok? Remember, life could be over in a second! Why on Earth should you waste your time doing things you don't like...or even hate? That's why I want to go through every aspect of your life to get super clear on what you want!

Imagine this big fat vision, like a lighthouse in your future. It shines its light on your sea of life and you are on your way to getting there. My goal of this book is to help you realize that YES, girl, YOU are the captain of your life, and you can be and do and have whatever you want.

One-Hundred-Year-Old You, Sitting on the Porch, Looking Back on Your Life

Ready for some time travels? I have a meditation on the book-bonus page ready for you to make this experience a real, 3D-movie, if you want. I love guided meditations, where you really see and feel things, where you can gain clarity and connect with your deepest truth. Get the meditation at: www.joyismycompass.com/bookbonus

If you are not into meditating right now, you can do this exercise just by reading this text and thinking it through.

So imagine you are one hundred years old. You are full of energy and in great shape, physically and mentally. You are shining. You are relaxed and wide awake at the same time. You just feel amazing, strong, and happy. You're sitting on your porch, balcony, or in your garden or...where are you? Imagine this situation, where you feel totally comfortable because this is YOUR future self, sitting there. Are you at the beach? In the mountains? Is the air hot and humid or cool and fresh? Ask yourself: Where am I?

Choose your dream destination and the conditions you feel best in, then close your eyes as your one-hundred-year-old self and look back on your life. You feel grateful for everything you've experienced and achieved. You might be moved by the trouble you went through, but you made it through, and it shaped you. You feel deep in your heart how powerful you've always been on your journey. Let your mind wander in your memories.

Where did you travel? Near and far? Did you go to the places you had always wanted to?

What did you do for a living? I'm sure you didn't have a job you hated. You did so many things and influenced others around you. Maybe you invented things, changed jobs, or built companies.

With whom did you spend your time? Do you have a partner? Do you have kids? Grandkids? Dogs? Other pets?

Imagine your friendships, those ladies and gentlemen you adore and hopefully still cherish... just let your mind wander and explore these precious memories.

How did you live, and where do you live now?

Just think of the rich and fulfilling life you had. And hey, it's not over yet, you still have many possibilities: To go on a yoga retreat in Bali, to go on a road trip with your grandchildren... you are so fit and healthy, you feel ready for more years to live on YOUR own terms, with all the people in your life you love.

Everybody around you calls you "the lucky lady", but you know it wasn't luck; it was YOUR work and purposefulness, it was you creating this life because that's how you wanted it. It feels *so* good. You have a big smile on your face and feel deeply grateful for everything that was possible. If you believe in God or the Universe or some bigger force, you give thanks to whom it may concern.

How did that feel? Good? Overwhelming? Did your mind comment on your images like, "That's not possible! What are you talking about? Are you kidding me?"

Tell your brain to take a break!

One friend, when I told her about this exercise, screamed, "One hundred? Are you crazy? At eighty years I'm done and OUT!"

Okaaay... I never thought about it that way. Unlike her, I want to stay in the game as long as possible. I know that today or tomorrow my game of life could be over, but my plans and my vision, they go beyond one hundred, for sure. We can't decide how old we'll get (of course, we technically *can* decide "it's over" and commit suicide, but I sincerely hope that's not an option for you!). If we want to stay vibrantly alive for as long as possible, we can help ourselves to become that one-hundred-year-old powerful lady by looking after ourselves and taking good care of our body and our mind. That's my plan, and I'm glad you joined me. I like it here. I like this world. I like everybody I meet. I like YOU! I love spending time with you in this book. Maybe we'll meet in person someday, somewhere. Everything is possible. Do you believe me? Do you hear me? Everything is possible—but first, you have to know what you want. So let's find out what you want!

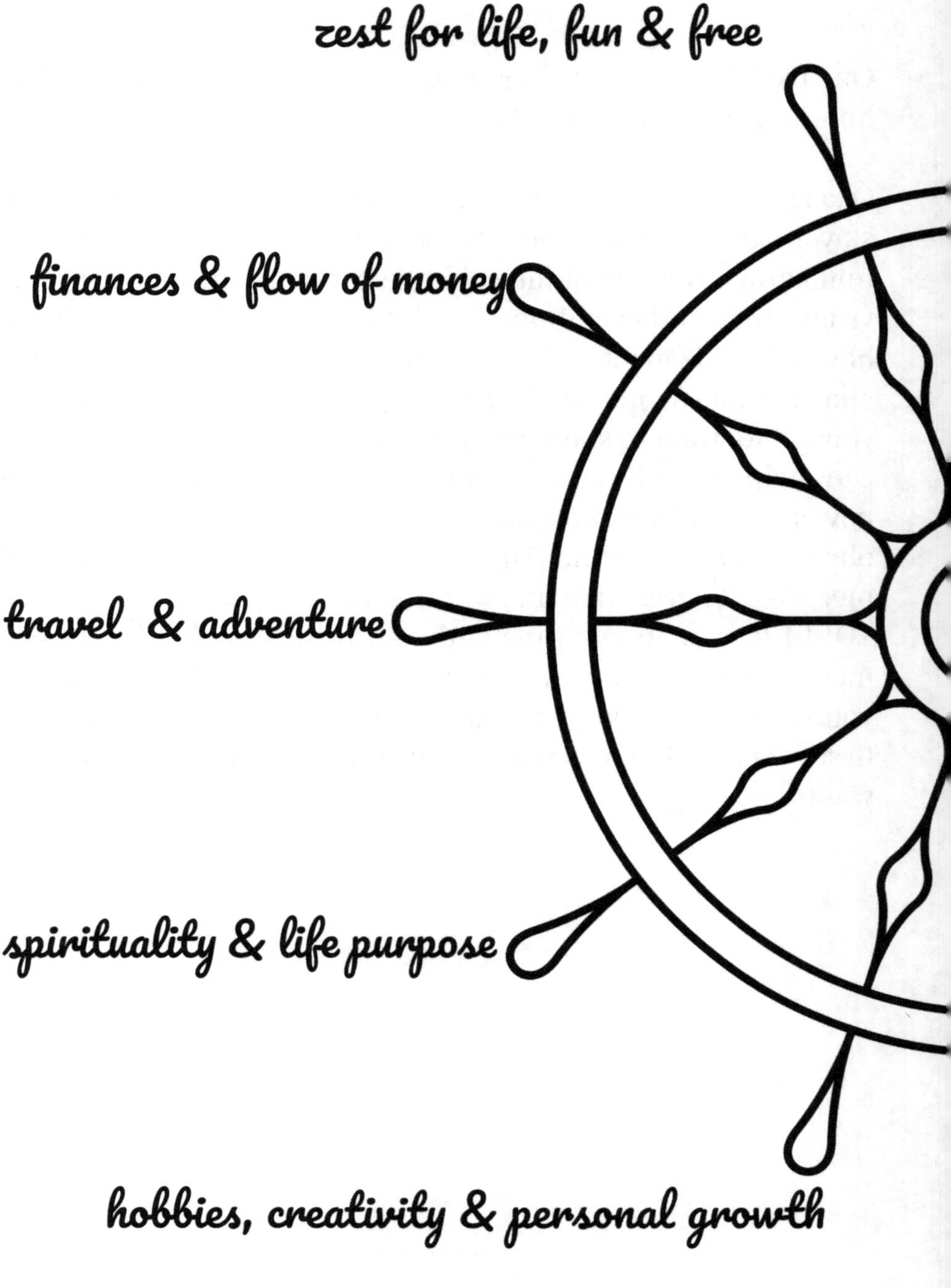

zest for life, fun & free
finances & flow of money
travel & adventure
spirituality & life purpose
hobbies, creativity & personal growth

love life & romance

family, friends
& relationship

living space,
physical

health, physical fitness,
relaxation & wellness
food & nurture

daily job, career & business

Your Personal Wheel Of Life

Have you heard of the wheel of life? It's a super simple tool that breaks your life down into categories. I have ten categories on mine, but you can customize it to your personal life.

First, find out: WHERE am I NOW? Be super super honest with yourself, even if it might hurt to admit how much of a mess your life is right now. Where are you in all these different categories, at this moment? As soon as you reveal where you're at, you can decide where you want to go.

Daily Job, Career, Business

Let's start with an easy topic! How much do you like what you're doing for a living? Ooh, okay...not so much? Your work sucks? No fun at all? Only weekends are fun? Monday, Tuesday, Wednesday, Thursday, Friday—five days are just horrible? Oh, you don't have a corporate job? You have kids? You work 24/7 with little bosses (sometimes terrorists) chasing you around the house? Or, oh, do you work part-time, and everything is just too much with family and kids?

I don't know your situation. Only YOU know it. On a scale of one to ten, how would you rate your daily job/career/business? If you are a stay-at-home mom, that's a fulltime job too, don't dismiss this and say, "I don't work."

Rate your work from one to ten.

Next question: WHY did you rate it this high or low?
What is shitty about it? And what is wonderful?

Write it all down. Describe the shittiness and wonderfulness in great detail. Let it all out! It feels so good to get all the crushed and suppressed feelings out on paper, doesn't it? Just see it as a fact. At the moment, this is your shitty, wonderful work life. No judgement. Take a deep breath!

The goal should be that you jump out of bed in the morning because you love what you do. That's my opinion, no exaggeration. You can change everything you hate right now and get some help if it's just too much for one person to handle. I know, you might think, "Yeah? And what about the money? I don't have the money to pay a housekeeper or a babysitter or work one less job…"

The fact is, if you are in a job- or career- or home-situation that you hate, something, someday, will wake you up and get you on your road again. Why wait? **Let's turn this ride around, so that you can enjoy what you're doing and feel satisfied in the evening with what you've accomplished.** Yes, this IS POSSIBLE! Yes, with ANY kind of education. Yes, you'll make enough money with your dream job. You'll make more money than ever by doing what you love and what you're good at!

"But my dad expects me to be a lawyer."
"But I would be a bad mother if I worked."
"I don't want to disappoint anyone."

Really? Is it better to punish yourself every day with a job you hate?

A job is a huge mix of expectations you have of yourself, expectations from your family, your boss, your coworker, and your kids, and what you actually do. The questions you have to ask yourself are:

- Do I like my job (by "job," I always mean any main activity you do throughout your day)?
- What do I like about my job?
- What do I dislike?
- What would I love to do for a living if I could choose freely, and money was not an issue?
- What am I really good at? Think about *everything* you're good at!
- What do I like doing? Think of *anything* you enjoy doing!
- Do I like to work with people? If yes, how? If no, what would be your preferred work setting?

You can decide what you want to do for work. The problem with doing something you hate or dislike or you're not interested in at all is, as I told you before: You'll get sick, or very unhappy, or you'll have one of these trendy burnouts—or did you hear about bore outs? That's when you are overwhelmed with the boring job you're doing day in and out! Whatever happens, you WILL get a wake-up call, an overwhelming need to change. Don't wait until you crash. Make the change now.

Ah, you are already unhappy? You feel burned out? You find your job so annoying that you hate Sunday night and Monday morning is even worse?

Maybe this is the time to change things.

Living five awful days per week is quite a shitty rate of good times versus bad times.
Maybe instead you're saying, "Hey, I can't change my work! I need this work to pay my bills!"

Don't quit your job today with no plan in your pocket. Think about the questions below NOW and write down all your thoughts!

What do I like about my job right now? What do I enjoy? What's working? What do I want to have in any job I'm doing?

What do I dislike about my job right now? What's the problem? What would I change TODAY if I could? What do I need to change, so that I can get up in the morning and look forward to going to work? If you are taking care of the home, the exact same questions apply.

I, for example, hate housework. I'm really not good in these kinds of jobs, and I don't enjoy them AT ALL except for cooking (but could somebody please clean up the kitchen after me?). My husband, Ken, and I are a really good team at home, and he cleaned more than I did in the household department for years. When Ken opened a restaurant with friends, I was thrilled that he finally designed his dream job without stupid bosses chasing him around. I agreed to take care of our kid more than ever before, because his work hours were long and he would come home after midnight almost every night.

He warned me that I practically wouldn't see him for the first six months. I agreed because I love restaurants. I loved to work in restaurants myself, and I really thought that his job-happiness is super important. I also felt that Zurich needed his cool, Japanese izakaya Restaurant (check www.ooki.tokyo).

Well, after about two months in, I was exhausted. I worked part-time as a teacher, part-time I was building my business, and all of a sudden, I had a full-time job with our little lady Mika, plus all this housework I hated so much

MY BIG FAT VISION

that used to be my husband's was now my job, too.

My husband is Japanese, and in Japan, NOBODY pays to have their house cleaned. Just the thought that someone would hold the keys to our apartment was super scary to Ken. His philosophy is: Clean up your own mess! In Japanese schools, kids clean the hallway, the cafeteria, their classrooms. When I was working in Japan, every Friday we wiped the floors, and once a month we worked around the factory building and pulled weeds out of the flowerbeds. So, a cleaning service was a no-go...but not anymore, with the restaurant in the game plan!

I was so angry that I had all these stupid things to do on top of my work and childcare, so I was DONE. I told Ken that he could do whatever he wanted, but I was booking a cleaning service, no matter what! He was so exhausted himself that he didn't say anything against it. We've had our cleaning angel for over three years now. She loves cleaning...it's like meditating, she says (are you CRAZY?), and now, every week after she is here, I message her a love-note and thank her for her work. I really do that. Delegating this task and seeing how she did it with so much love and care for our living space is so, so beautiful! Sometimes I'm moved to tears. No kidding.

What I want to say: There are things you hate to do. There are things you are not good at. Delegating and outsourcing is the solution. A big chunk of money goes away every month for us to have a cleaning lady. In Switzerland, salaries are very high—but it's worth every penny if I think about the time it would take for me to clean and the amount of energy I would waste because I would be so upset about doing this work. We now happily transfer money over to the lady who loves to do this job. How AWESOME is that?!

On top of this wonderful change, I told my darling husband that I'd take care of Mika in the morning and the evening because he's either not here or very tired. We tried to share this task, but he was too grumpy in the morning and I understood that. Being sleep-deprived is not fun at all. I wanted our kid to go to school after a harmonious morning without yelling or stress, so I took over this part of the family work. In return, the whole laundry business is now Ken's job. What a glorious life I have now. I only do what I love at home (besides cleaning the kitchen after my chaotic cooking!) and the rest of the tasks are outsourced and delegated.

You might think: "Hey, you! We are talking about how I rate my work from one to ten, and you're talking about a cleaning lady and delegating the laundry to your husband?"

    MY BIG FAT VISION

YES! Everything is intertwined and connected. I work both from home and from my office, which is within walking distance. I take care of Mika in the morning and in the evening with some exceptions, and I cook lunch for her three times a week (the Swiss school system is still stuck in medieval times, and kids come home for lunch because mothers are at home, right...?). To be fair, our school is three minutes away, and all the kids walk there. For two days, she stays at school the whole day. Sometimes my husband is at home to prepare lunch, so that's an extra workday for me. That's how my work setting looks. I quit teaching after twelve years, and now I'm my own boss at my company RonjaSakata.com where I offer my Joy Academy workshops, coach awesome clients and do public speaking. I love to work alone in my office and be on stage. I love my flexibility. I love that I can work AND take care of my girl the way I want.

If you had told me about my current reality five years ago, I wouldn't believe one word! I would have said, "No way. I will teach forever! My business will stay a side gig. No way will I make enough money from my business to quit teaching."

Ask yourself: What do I LIKE, what do I LOVE about my work (again, Mama, if you are staying at home taking care of your home-business, you can think through these questions too!)? What do I HATE, what do I DISLIKE about my work?

**What do I want to change? Delegate? Outsource?
How would my ideal work situation look, if anything
could be possible?**

Maybe you actually don't want another job right now, and quitting and starting somewhere new is too scary? That's okay, too!

Maybe you could change your attitude, instead of your job? Could I show up with more presence? How would that be? How do I want to present myself, anyway?

How could I do my job with more excellence? How would I be different, if I gave my everything to my current job?

Imagine your work as a cool place to go, where you're having a blast, doing what you like with nice people, and in the evening you're really happy with your day! If you are at home with your kids, this applies, too!

Mika, my daughter, recently hit the nail on the head: "Mama, you told me that we can choose our mood. Why are you so grumpy then?" Oh wow... here she comes, holding up the mirror. I laughed and told her, "Okay, let's choose a better mood. But you too, okay?"

Before her comment, we were arguing with each other, and I felt rushed with preparing dinner and getting the girl to bed early. Thanks to her, we then had a fun, harmonious evening. We can choose our mood. We can choose our attitude. This is ALWAYS a lot easier if we sleep enough and if our self-care game is strong. We'll get to that later in the book.

Let's create a life that suits us, which we love! I like to think of life as a big playground where I can choose everything on my behalf: My mood, my attitude, my actions, my way of interacting with the creatures and things around me. I also get to choose my job, and since that takes up so many hours a day, that choice better be a good one!

Ask yourself: What would I adore to do for a living if I could choose freely and money would not be an issue?

Think about any activity you love, that you would love to earn money with. We are living in internet times... we have the best opportunities to earn money with anything we can think of. The world waits at your doorstep... or, more truthfully, in your computer. If you're not thinking of an online career, even offline jobs are brilliantly supported by the internet for connecting, producing, printing, reporting ... the possibilities are endless. Think about everything you're good at! Write them all down. Think of anything you enjoy doing. You might create your new job, right here and now!

- Do I like to work with people? If yes, how? If no, what would be your preferred work setting?
- Do I like to create something to sell? Do I like to teach, support, connect?

Write about your dream job. Note ideas, activities, and things you'd love to do. Do some brainstorming, and hang the ideas on the fridge.

What kind of work do you want to do?

Dream about it. Imagine working at your new dream job before you fall asleep at night.

Imagine yourself doing the coolest most awesome job ever, earning a ton of money while having fun. During the day, don't compare your current job with your dream job. Don't complain. Do your work with a new commitment, new power and new energy.

Try to not complain about anything for a week, and notice the difference in you (this is a big one, and not so easy, but go for it. This is a game-changer)!

Try to go all-in at work for a week, and you'll feel totally different the next Monday morning. Nothing changed except how you think about your work. I love that. It's free, it's working, it's a decision you can make in one second.

I bet your boss will recognize the difference (and if your boss is your toddler, he or she will notice the difference, too!). Maybe your coworkers will be annoyed that you are happyhappyallday all of a sudden. They'll get over it, and step by step you'll influence them without saying a word!

You never know if, by changing your attitude, your current job will turn into your dream job. Or maybe you will get an offer within your company to do another job. Whatever will happen, I promise you that your chances for promotion or other good things are at least a million percent up, now that you changed your work attitude. Do you agree? Can you see my point?

I think we nailed the job-spoke of the wheel of life now. You did a great job thinking and dreaming about how you want to earn your money in the future.

"Sometime… Eventually… If possible…" There is not much momentum in these statements, huh? So, what do you do to make these dreams come true? If you do something every day, you'll reach your goal for sure. You go, girl! In the job-career department, wherever you work, however you feel right now, you've got this! Your dream job is out there, go and get it or go and create it!

Family / Relationships And Love Life / Romance

Shall we tackle another big topic?...
From one to ten, where are you on these two spokes: family/relationships and love life/romance? Generally speaking, on the whole?

Let's say you have a brilliant guy in your life, who is super confident, doing his own thing. Spending time with him is fun and easy. You can make fun of each other and have deep conversations. You spend lots of quality time together, and you do things alone or with your own peers. You both go for big goals in life and support each other in achieving them.

Let's say you have kids together, and you love them. They trust you, you trust them, and together you are the family gang. You back up each other no matter what. Your home is filled with laughter and fun. You all communicate openly and with great respect for each other. It's just so wonderful to be the Mama of this clan!

Let's say you have a great relationship with your parents, and you admire them for their legacy. Your siblings are your cheerleaders, and you all take care of each other.

Did you nod and smile and say, "YEP, that's my reality" ...or did you hate me for this paragraph?

How IS your reality?

- Are you single, desperately looking for your "other half"?
- Are you single, and very happy that you don't have anybody to take care of?
- Do you have a relationship, and it's a constant disaster?

I know, I mentioned all the stereotypes and extremes... only you know what is going on in your relationship-department. Only *you* can be honest with yourself, as in the job discussion: How am I doing here? And WHAT do I want?

What did you think when you read the "ideal" family situation above? Did you say, "Uuuuh, I can't stand this Hollywood-trash!" Were you thinking, "Oh yeah, that's a nice dream, but not possible for me?"

While discussing your job situation, I could say, "Go find a job you love! Go and do your current job really well, while you go step by step toward your dream job or business!" But relationships are much more complicated. Much more diverse. You can be a lone wolf and LOVE it, or you can be in the same situation and very lonely and desperate.

Wherever you are on your journey through your life, and however your relationships and your love life are:
WHAT do you want?!

Write that down. Take out your journal and write down HOW you want to rule this spoke of your wheel of life!

You can ask yourself similar questions as in your work-situation:

What do I like about my love life right now? What's working in my relationships? What am I grateful for? What makes me happy?

First, focus on what's going well. Write down even the smallest things you're grateful for. That's something I want to train you to do throughout this book. Focusing on the positive things (even though you're aware of what is shitty and miserable) is better than focusing on everything that's wrong.

Can you get a notebook and write? I mean it! Writing things down is like free therapy. We can bring our thoughts in order and see things clearer than before.

So, ask yourself again: What do I like about my love life right now? What works great in my relationships? What am I grateful for? What makes me happy? What's working?
WRITE your answers down!

Now, what do you hate about what's going on in your relationships? In your love life? What do you want to change?

What can you change?

The good news: You can only change yourself and nobody else.
The bad news: You can only change yourself and nobody else.

Ha, ha... not funny? It's just a fact! I think it's a good one, too! Taking full responsibility for yourself and only yourself is much easier than taking responsibility for everyone around you. If you are fully aware of this fact, you can focus only on YOU! How do I speak with people around me? How do I treat people around me (your spouse, your boyfriend, your friends, your kids, your neighbors, and the random folks you meet at the supermarket)?

How do I want to BE in my relationships? How do I want to play the game of life within my family and in my love life? What do I think of others? How do I judge others? How do I talk to myself in my thoughts? How do I judge myself?

Lots of things to think about, right?
What do you want?

Write YOUR ideal situation down, even though you might think that this is never gonna happen. "This only happens to others, not me" ... Nope! Everything is possible. YOU can change YOU, and that's enough to change everything around you. Cool?

Your notebook should be full of notes by now. Don't read any further before you've done your journaling! To change things, you need to work on things! You need to do your homework for yourself.

What do I want to change in my relationship-game? Can I be more present? Can I listen better? Can I just give my love a big bear hug instead of arguing over the same things as always? Can I say clearly what I need and want, to have the relationship I wish for? Do I know what I want? How would my relationships change if I step up my game and bring JOY into it?

Choose the questions that you like best, and write about them!

Take some time off for thinking and writing. You don't have time? Switch off your TV and put the phone down. I'm sure you'll find time, now! And hey, it's *so* worth it! I can't wait to hear from you, how you're ROCKING it and how happy you are that you did this journaling, because the journaling was the beginning of changing YOU and with that, your surroundings slowly changed along.

Next?

For the next spokes of the wheel of life, you don't need me to outtalk you. In every topic, ask yourself: What's the current state of my life in this area? How would I rate this topic from one to ten? And, super important, WHY? Think about the reasons why you gave you this rating! This is so eye-opening. WHY are you not happy, why are you angry, or the opposite: Why are you giving yourself a nine out of ten? These reasons are so cool to realize, good and bad! Just journal, and watch what comes to your mind!

We'll talk a lot about your living space and physical environment in the next chapter. We'll tackle health, wellness, physical fitness, and food in the self-care section of the book. For the remaining topics, I'm throwing in these questions:

What do you want to do in your free time for your personal fun? How do you bring your zest for life to a new level? Where do you want to travel? What kind of adventure do you want to experience before you die? What do you want to learn? Skydiving? Rock climbing? Cooking? Crocheting? Are you creative, but don't give yourself time for it? Do you love woodcarving? Gardening? Painting? Music? What is your life's purpose? What do you want to leave behind when you're gone? What shall be your legacy? And hey, how much money do you want to make? More than what you make now? Millions? Billions? Everything is possible!

You don't believe me? Let's proceed!

I have two very cool and easy exercises ready for you to do to get even clearer about what you want. "No," you're saying. "No more questions, please!" Okay, got it. No more questions. Maybe.

Let's take a closer look at your dream life, the dream you might never have thought about because you learned as a kid: Don't talk about your dreams...

Be-Do Have

This exercise is so much fun!

It means that you think about what you want to BE, what you want to DO and what you want to HAVE in your life. It's like writing a wish list to Santa:

Just check in with yourself. Ask yourself what you want to be, and write it ALL down.

- I want to be happy and successful.
- I want to be strong.
- I want to be fit and healthy.
- I want to be a New York Times best-selling author.
- I want to be in a thriving relationship.
- I want to be a house owner of my dream house.

NEXT: What do you want to DO in your life?
Not "I want to do awesome things." Be more specific:

- I want to do lots of sports every day.
- I want to write a book.
- I want to win a certain competition.
- I want to run a marathon.
- I want to build my business into an international enterprise.

What do you want to do in your life, specifically, from morning to evening...?

What do you want to do as your hobbies, in your job, in your family...whatever comes to your mind:

What do you want to DO?

The last one, HAVE, can be materialistic or an achievement:

- I want to have a great relationship with my parents (or kids, or partner).
- I want to have a BMW, 320Ci Cabriolet...
- I want to have a big house (and describe it in great detail, because you don't want just any old big house, you want to have the big house YOU like).

Please check in with your HAVE–list and only write things down, which make YOU happy. If you want to impress your neighbors and play keeping up with the Joneses, it will not make you happy in the long run. Write down only what YOU desire and want and will have in your life!

Everything is possible, just write it down!

Do you know what the difference is between a millionaire and a billionaire? The billionaire writes down his goals twice a day.
I heard that quote from Denise Duffield-Thomas, a self-made, Australian millionaire who is a big inspiration to thousands of women. You might know one of her books: *Get Rich, Lucky Bitch*? If not, this is a GOOD one to read in order to get clear about your money mindset. My favorite one of hers is *Chillpreneur*. If you have your own business, please read this one. It's brilliant.

Writing down your goals is a game-changer if you want to be a millionaire or just have a better life for you and your family. By writing down what you want to Be-Do-Have, you have your dreams and goals always at the top of your mind. You are always thinking about them in a good way. Your focus is sharpened, and you'll be aware of sudden opportunities, see chances, and stumble over signs you didn't recognize before.

What's important is that you write down your Be-Do-Have list while you're in a good mood. It should be fun, and you should feel great, like, "Hell YEAH, THIS is my future! It's a done deal, I'm getting everything on my list!"

I want you to write a Be-Do-Have for right now. What do you wish for NOW? Remember, you can decide to change it in an instant. So, if you write down: I want to have a great relationship with my parents; you are aware of this goal. Maybe you'll just call them, or go and say hi. Maybe you always fight, and it's always a mess? This time, you could just listen and give your Mama a big hug. YOU know what you can change and how you can behave differently to change things, just because you've decided to do so. Don't rush. If you have old family patterns that have been running for decades, you might need some time. But only your decision to have a great relationship with your parents (or any person who is important to you) can change things for the better in BIG ways. Try it!

Some things need time, so I want you to write another list for "in five years" and another one for "in ten years." You'll see how your goals might get bigger because you believe that you can make it happen within ten years. Some wishes never change, like the I-want-to-be-happy or I-want-to-be-successful wishes. These are things you can achieve right now by changing your attitude and by how you show up at work and by how you interact with the important people around you.

Always write down the date of the day you wrote the list. It's so cool when you read through old lists and you can see: CHECK, CHECK, CHECK. You will be amazed by what you've already accomplished! It's really wild, what's possible as soon as you are open to thinking about what you want and then going for it!

Your work:
- Write down a Be-Do-Have for right now or this year
- Write down a Be-Do-Have for in five years (note the year you're referring to on the list, i.e., if you write this list in 2020, write on the top "In 2026")
- Write down a Be-Do-Have for in ten years (and note the year, as well)

Remember the millionaire and billionaire quote? You decide how often you play around with this exercise. Daily? Weekly? Monthly? I suggest to do it as many times as possible, but it should be FUN, and not an obligation.

Like I said, it should feel great! Playful! Fun! Feel the goals, feel the things you'll have, see the house and the car... yeah, maybe this sounds corny, but just do it anyway! You'll see the evidence very soon that this journaling exercise is worth its weight in GOLD.

My Ideal Day

Did you do the Be-Do-Have? No? Go and do it, please!... If you don't put in the effort, nothing will change! It's like push-ups. Thinking of push-ups won't make you stronger. You have to actually DO them.

What's your ideal day? If you have your Be-Do-Have in your mind, this will be an easy thing to write out. Why do double the work? Because it's a different approach, and we have to use many different approaches to convince your subconscious mind that all your dreams are possible. You have to change your mindset to the "achiever and winner" mindset. You have to get rid of your complaining, moaning, bitching, gossiping, and making fun of others and instead put all this energy into what you want to achieve and become.

You don't have to; you can stay exactly as you are...but if you DECIDE to change, the more power to you!

The ideal day exercise goes like this:
Imagine, you wake up, eyes still closed. Where are you? "In a bed, of course..." No, I mean where are you sleeping? In a hammock in a bungalow in Costa Rica? In a king size bed in your mansion? Really imagine this situation, and play around with the gazillions of possibilities, even still half asleep and with your eyes closed. What are you wearing? Are you naked? Are you wearing a shiny, millionaire, silky pajama? Is there somebody next to you? Is there a baby's leg in your face? What would be the perfect, ideal wake-up situation? What do you hear? Waves? Is the window open? Do you feel the breeze? Then open your eyes and look around. Again, where are you? How does this room or place look? Is it your home? Is it your hotel room on your vacation?

I did this exercise with students at a university in Switzerland, and I gave them fifteen minutes to write. I was unsure if they would like or hate it. After fifteen minutes, I stopped them, and one guy yelled, "Hey, don't interrupt me! I didn't even get out of bed yet!" That was a nice confirmation that this journaling prompt can be so much fun.

Go all in! Write down all the details: What time did you get up? Did you set your alarm? What does the flooring look like? Fluffy carpet? Wood? Are you wearing slippers? Are you barefoot? Think of it like a movie that you can change within seconds with just your thoughts. Design your whole day in this way. What's next? What do I want to do next in my ideal perfect day? What do I eat for breakfast? Did somebody prepare it for me?

In my personal ideal day I have a very nice staff. I only do the tasks I love to do, like cooking, but cleaning, that's not my job anymore. My staff has super high salaries, and we treat them like kings and queens. They do their job just perfectly. They love to work at our house. It's a total win–win situation. That's how I want to shape my future. How do you want yours?

What will you do next? A workout? Paragliding? Wakeboarding? Dog training? Bring your kids to their awesome school? Go to your dream workplace? What do you do for a living? Where is your money coming from? Real estate?

At a conference held by Brendon Burchard (check him out, he is one of my heroes who influenced me profoundly) I met Mike, a very charming guy. I asked him, "What do you do for work?"

"Oh, I have a real estate business. But the business works best if I'm not around. My staff does a great job, so I stay out of their way. I travel all year round. In summer I'm in Europe, and in winter I'm in South Asia or South America."

I was so impressed—and inspired! I really don't want to travel all year round. I love to live in one place and travel sometimes. But I'm working toward my company becoming a really fun "machine" that can run with little time needed from my side, so I can only do what I love: Write, speak, coach, put out inspirational content and be creative with videos, paintings, drawings. That's my personal dream...

What is YOURS?

So how is your ideal day proceeding? What are you doing next? Spending the afternoon with your husband in a spa? Choose what you LOVE, what makes you HAPPY, what makes you smile and be in awe of your life—the life you created!

- What are you doing next?
- What are you eating?
- What do you do for your body?

- What do you do for fun?
- What's next? And then what?

Write yourself through your entire day until you go to bed again—or hop into your hammock, or your campervan. Include a recap of the day, laying in your bed, thinking through your day. Be grateful for all the things you were able to Be-Do-Have. Say thank you to whomever you believe in, or say thank you to yourself for being awesome today! For giving your best! For enjoying your blessings.

DONE!

You can write an ideal day for the end of this year, for in five years or ten years again. It's super interesting to see, like in the Be-Do-Have list, how you think differently and what you give yourself credit for achieving. Dream BIG. For the ideal day by the end of this year, you might just add a cleaning person and your husband might be doing the laundry. Wouldn't that be the BEST thing ever to have in your ideal day? Of course, that's just an example, but YOU know best. What do you dare to wish for in a short amount of time? For the ten-year version, please don't hold back. Write down ANYthing you would love to have or do in your ideal day. Have FUN!

What do you think about this exercise? Why bother? Never going to happen anyway?

Don't stay in Stuckville. Do you know Stuckville? I heard of it from Leonie Dawson (check her out) and I loved the analogy. You might live there right now. You might have rented a condo there, but PLEASE don't build a house in Stuckville. Go ON with your life and try something new. I know, you might not like journaling, or find it exhausting, or just stupid. Just get over it and DO IT.

If you did the exercise and loved it, Stuckville is far away for you.

Journaling is magic. I promise. It's pure magic flowing out of your pen and onto paper. You'll be amazed by yourself and your thoughts and how quickly you'll change. Not for being a "good girl", not for impressing your parents or neighbors or anybody you might have had to impress in your childhood. No! Just for YOU! You being proud of yourself and your life is the greatest gift you can give yourself. But first, you have to know what you WANT! And by doing all the things in this (very long) chapter, you'll figure it out. Ready for some decluttering? Let's check out the next chapter. You are in this with me together. You will benefit from all these things we're doing together! Just read and DO THE WORK! And remember, I love you!

DECLUTTERING ON THE OUTSIDE

Only What You Love Is Allowed to Stay

Before you come home, before you even enter...what are you thinking? As you push the door open, what goes through your mind? Nothing? Or are you thinking, "Urgh, here it comes, my messy home, where random things are lying around in layers." Is it the complete opposite? "Home sweet home, you are my castle and I'm the queen!"

I don't know anything about your living space, but you do!

I'm sure you've heard about people who wanted to sell their house, and to sell it, they have to do a big decluttering session.

They paint the fence in a fresh color. The old dead plants in front of the house get replaced by new ones, and so on. The goal is that the pics of the house look *very good* for the sales page. But then they realize how stupid they were for living all these years in a place with dead plants in front of the house and a huge mess inside. Turns out that old house wasn't so ugly after all—it just needed a little love.

You (and your family) deserve to live in a place that makes you happy and proud. You *can* decide to go all-in and make yourself comfortable at home. You can create a space you are proud of and love spending time in.

Do you like to have visitors at your home? If not, it's probably because you think it's not elegant enough, not nice enough, not clean enough, not styled enough. We have these kinds of thoughts because we are always comparing things to friends or other people who have fancy houses or living spaces. Forget about the others; let's concentrate on you, shall we?

You can live in a one-room apartment, in a tiny house, in a camper van, or in a mansion. Wherever you live, you are responsible for your happiness at home. Do you own the fact by now that you are responsible for your whole life? OWN this responsibility. It's an honor to take care of yourself and your surroundings.

I'm not a neat person at all. By the time I was a teenager, my mother gave up, and we had one rule left for my room: "Keep the door closed!"

The problem is, I'm still messy, and I have to put a lot of effort into keeping my space tidy. Ken is perfect compared to me, and it's annoying how good he is! Our daughter has the same chaotic character as me, so he's outnumbered and whines sometimes that he is the unluckiest guy with us messy ladies.

When I have guests I always clean up. It annoys me that I do this for friends, but not for myself. Do you know that feeling? It's the same when I keep the promises I made to everybody else, but not the ones I made to myself. Grrrrr... but again, only I can change that one.

So, how about you promise yourself to live in a place you admire, that you are proud of, and where you feel totally in your power? Sound good?

It's funny for me to think about your home without even having been to your place. Maybe you have the most gorgeous house, where everything is just picture-perfect, and I am here trying to talk with you about decluttering. Maybe your home *looks* beautiful, but only you know about the millions of things hidden in the cupboards that you don't want to think about. Maybe you have a tidy house, but your garage is filled to the brim with "stuff"? Maybe not. Whatever your situation, just stay with me and take away what speaks to you, okay?

My reason to talk you into the decluttering-topic is the big point of this book: YOU deserve a life where you just think, "Wow, okay, never thought that would ever be possible." Your living space is where you sleep, where you rest, where you spend time with your family and friends, where you cook...so it's really super helpful when you feel GREAT at home!

The second month of my Joy Mastermind Program is focused on decluttering because I really believe the impact of a beautiful environment makes all the other life changes so much easier. First comes vision, then decluttering. These two topics are the basis of all the inner work that follows. How cool is that? You get a big portion of my life-transforming, five-month program all in this one book! If you do the work, which I'm sure you'll do, you will be a different person after reading all these pages!

In my five-month-long group coaching program called Joy Mastermind, I once had a client who felt completely trapped in an apartment that was not big enough for herself and her three kids, and she wanted to move to a bigger place badly. All the things in her space felt overwhelming and energy-sucking. She went all-in with our decluttering month, threw out a ton of things, and

get out the snowboard jacket from the attic, or clothes you have in your garage, your basement. Just get them OUT and throw them in the middle of your living room or bedroom. It can be overwhelming to see the sheer amount of clothes that you own. Maybe you'll realize you only use twenty percent of them. Or even less!

Now is the chance to clean out your closet, because it's empty. Once that's done, go to the mountain of clothes, and start on the top of the pile. Take one t-shirt and ask yourself, "Does it spark joy?"

DON'T ask yourself: Does this fit me? Shall I wear this again? Is it still good? That's the trap of keeping things just because we "should" or because your mother told you to buy this or your friend gifted it to you.

Does it make you happy? Yes or no? Or maybe?

The yes-pile goes neatly back into your closet again.
The no-pile goes to the thrift shop or homeless shelter or wherever you can make a ton of people happy with the clothes you don't want anymore.
The maybe-pile is actually the no-pile, because, come on, if you don't make it to the yes-pile, you're OUT! (So true everywhere in life, right?)

When I did my internship in Japan in 2001, I had to go to work in a suit! I was a student back then and didn't own one pant suit and, for sure, no skirt. So, I bought three sets of suits and lots of blouses to combine for four months of going to work daily. I looked so well-behaved. I kept these suits for ages because I thought that I could reuse them one day. I was the jeans and t-shirt type of girl, and if it was cold, a hoodie kept me warm. In 2012, when Mika was two years old, I had enough of my style. I was terrified of buying a dress or some more feminine clothes, yet I wanted a change. So, I booked a professional style consultant who my sister highly recommended. She was so nice. She kept a poker face when looking through my clothes. She was very professional, and told me, "Okay, I see. You have lots of jeans, t-shirts, and hoodies. Those suits, no way you can use them, they are... um... they have to go."

We went shopping the next week, and it was such an eye-opener. I told her I like bold colors, and she listened to that. Still, she didn't listen to my concerns that my legs look like very white elephant legs and that the muscles of my calves are too big and belong to a soccer player. She got very firm when she told me, "Your legs are perfect!" She didn't tell me to shut up, but her tone of voice told me to get over myself, now! This was very short, but very effective "therapy." Since that day, I wear dresses all the time, and I made peace with my soccer player's legs. I even accept my nearly see-through white skin tone. I got rid of the suits and imagined somebody in the thrift shop being delighted to have the possibility to buy a neat suit for an interview or something serious. Now, as I write this book nine years later, I still have dresses I bought with the style consultant. My favorite one is now a very light coral red instead of a bold coral...and unfortunately, the fabric is ripped at the armhole. It still sparks so much joy for me, so I still have it. It reminds me of this "transformation." I'll find out when it's time for it to go when it no longer brings a smile to my face.

That's why I like this KonMari Method so much. It doesn't tell you to only keep the good and throw out the old and shabby things. It teaches you what you love and what you WANT, and that's the big question we're solving on so many levels throughout this book: What do I want? And then once we know that, go and get it!

Don't think that you can delegate this work. YOUR stuff is YOUR stuff, and only YOU can sort it out. You are also NOT allowed to throw away things that belong to other people in your household. The things of your spouse, your kids, your grandmother (if she's still alive) are NOT your business. Don't touch your husband's or boyfriend's old, worn-down t-shirt. He might love it dearly, and if you throw it away without even asking that's a huge violation of his personal boundaries. Don't do that! Okay? If you want to get your guy into decluttering mode, just leave this book lying around with the men's cover facing up, which you can download on the book-bonus page. My challenge is to talk him into this topic. Tell me if I succeeded!

Ken and I always had our own room. Even when we only had a two-bedroom apartment. We decided which room is assigned to whom and made a golden rule: We were not allowed to comment on anything about each other's room: Decoration, furniture, pictures on the wall... it's MY room or HIS room. MY room was our office, and I had a ton of pictures of our friends and family on the wall. I had the closet for both of us in my room, so I got to choose the design at IKEA. Ken's room was our bedroom, and beside the bed, he had some locker-style furniture I really didn't like, but hey... no comments allowed.

We still live by that rule, even though we have a bigger apartment now. Mika, our daughter, has her room now too and is the boss in there. The living room, hallway, kitchen, and bathroom are middle ground space. Every new thing in there has to be approved by the democracy of our family. That's why we have a really bright, really bling-blingy lamp from the hardware store in our hallway. I got outvoted.

When I started using the KonMari Method for our living space, I started with my closet, and began to fold the t-shirts and sweatshirts as she recommends it. She says to put them upright, folded in little squares, into your drawers. That way you can see all your t-shirts right away.

No piles are hiding the ones at the very bottom. First, Ken commented that this is a stupid new thing to do (he is the laundry boss in our household, so he puts away the super neatly folded clothes)! And a week later, when I checked something in his closet, I saw he had applied the KonMari style to his t-shirts too!

So, you're working through your (gigantic?) pile of clothes yourself and only keep the things you love. Then, you put everything from the yes-pile back into your closet. If you've never heard about Marie Kondo before, she has a book, thousands of blogs, and a Netflix show explaining the way to fold and put away your clothes.

I like how Marie Kondo treats objects with great respect and love. That's a Japanese mindset I love so much. Ken takes such good care of ALL his things. In Shintoism, one of the two major religions in Japan, they believe that everything from a tree to a stone, a car to a toilet, has a god or goddess within. That's one of the reasons they treat everything so respectfully. When I once made spaghetti carbonara for my host family in Japan, I wanted to pour the hot pasta water into the sink. The mother jumped into the kitchen and yelled, "Don't upset the sink god!" *Ooooh my... there is even a sink god?* With lots of cold tap water combined, I was allowed to get rid of the boiling pasta water. Think about this story, every time you make pasta!

That's why I think saying thank you to your unwanted things is so beautiful. You thank them for the "work" they've done for you, and it addresses somehow the goddess that lives in this dress or t-shirt. I love this kind of mindful action. Anyway, bring away the carloads of clothes you don't want anymore. Don't let them sit in plastic bags in your hallway, okay? Out is out—and then, you'll feel the great feeling of accomplishment. I promise the energy will be different in your home after everything unwanted is gone! Even if it's only you doing this at the moment, your family will get the hang of it... just be patient!

Yes, we're only done with clothes, but now you know how this works!

There is a checklist for you on the book-bonus page where you can check off the different things to go through.

Imagine again, how you will feel when you enter your place, and you think, "Oh, my freaking God this is MY HOME!" Like when you enter a hotel room, and you are just in awe of the niceness of this place... Does this seem impossible for you? It's not! Just do it, wonderful lady. If you watch TV for hours or scroll through social media for days, put your priorities in line, turn off the electronics, and go and take care of your living space!

You might be a collector. You might have very small things, keepsakes you think you CAN'T ever throw away. Here comes the handy question again: Does it spark joy? Don't keep anything out of obligation. Don't put any gifts on display only when aunt so and so or this or that friend is coming over. NO. This is YOUR space, and if they cannot cope with you disliking what they have given you, that's NOT your problem. Period. Hurt feelings? NOT your problem. I prefer to be honest and nicely tell the truth: "Oh, that's nice, but I actually can't use this. Would you mind gifting it to someone who really needs this?" Do you think I'm rude? I think it's easier to say that right away instead of making things up until they hopefully forget.

Just keep things you love on display, or in a treasure-box somewhere. I'm very bad at letting things of this category go, but if you wait long enough, eventually you might think: Why the hell did I keep this for so long, when it's so easy to throw it out?

If your apartment or house is just a DREAM after going through all the corners, don't forget your basement or your attic or garage or garden house or storage place. You always remember the stuff there like, "No, in my storage are fifteen huge boxes and I don't even know what's in there..." Everything you own is connected to you, and if there are a ton of things in your life you own, and you don't even like them, they suck away your energy.

I hope that you are super motivated to do whatever needs to be done to create your living space in a way that makes you super happy, super proud, and super comfortable. That's the goal of all this work. Of course, it depends on your starting point. If you don't own so much stuff, you'll be done in a few days...or even hours? If you're in any way similar to me, you have a ton of things to work your way through.

Don't forget to decorate your space in the way you love it. If you didn't pay any attention to extras like decoration, think of what you would love to build-buy-create to make your space your OWN! This is not reserved for designers! You know what style you like, so get it into your home. If you live together with awesome people like your partner and kids, have a relaxed conversation about every room and how you could make it more comfortable, more unique, more personal, and more beautiful! Please consider yourself the VIP of your life. You deserve nice and beautiful things that bring you joy and make you happy.

As soon as you are done with all this decluttering and decorating, throw a party to celebrate you and your space with as many or as few people as you'd like. This was a great effort, maybe a team effort with your family. Own the fact that you are a superstar, and you are fully in your power. Say thank you to YOU, because only reading a book doesn't change anything. Actually doing the things the author is trying to persuade you into, that's really great. Congratulations and applause to you. You are Wonder Woman to me!

DECLUTTERING ON THE INSIDE

Free Yourself From Your Limitations

Now I know what your space looks like: It's beautiful, it's crispy clean, only things that make you happy surround you, and you feel like the queen that you are!

Let's go inside ourselves now and declutter all the thoughts, limiting beliefs, and negative self-talk, because all these things do NOT serve you at all. Let's change that and get very clear about what you want to kick out.

Let's also find out how you want to grow and what you want more of. It's all in our head, and it's invisible, so we can't just grab a thought and put it into a garbage bag, like a broken toy. But I do have some really awesome tools ready for you so that it *feels* like you threw those negative thoughts into the garbage bag... or even better. Let's get rid of these shitty thoughts that make us miserable.

The first tool is the idea of journaling alongside the MOON. I love the moon and how it "grows" and how it "gets smaller." When I was a child, my parents always sang a German lullaby called: *Der Mond ist aufgegangen* in the evening. The title means "The moon is risen." For the past nine years, I have also been singing two of the many verses to Mika every night:

> The moon is risen, beaming,
> The golden stars are gleaming
> So brightly in the skies;
> The hushed, black woods are dreaming,
> The mists, like phantoms, seeming,
> From meadows magically rise.
>
> Look at the moon so lonely
> One half is shining only,
> Yet she is round and bright;
> Thus, often we laugh unknowing
> At things that are not showing,
> That still are hidden from our sight.

   DECLUTTERING ON THE INSIDE

I love this part so much: "One half is shining only, yet she is round and bright."

The moon seems to grow and be full, and then get smaller and even as the thinnest crescent moon, we know that the moon is a perfect ball dashing around the earth. The new moon is called "empty moon" in German. No moon is visible... even though we know she's there.

"One half is shining only, yet she is round and bright; Thus, often we laugh unknowing, at things that are not showing, that still are hidden from our sight."

Let's look at the dark side of the moon within our thoughts, and don't laugh at them because they held us safe and small so far. At the same time, we use the beautiful moon as a reminder of our journaling practice. A perfect helper up there in the sky.

The next full moon will be our starting point: We, you and I will write down ALL THE THINGS we want to get rid of, what we want to let go, what is not serving us and just holding us back.

Write down everything limiting that comes to your mind, and you could even start the journaling as a letter to the full moon, that's more fun than only writing a list. Write it on a simple piece of paper and NOT in your beautiful journal. You'll see why.

Dear Full Moon

Thank you for helping me let go of all this shit I'm writing about to you in this letter. Thank you for this opportunity!

I want to let go of these thoughts:
- I am too fat.
- I am lazy.
- I am not good at anything.
- I am not interesting enough for others.
- I don't know what to say in social situations.
- Everybody else looks better, does better, is better...

... go on with this list, and of course, my examples may be completely wrong for you! But you get the point!

Continue writing with habits you want to get rid of:
- I want to stop saying mean and bad things about myself when I see myself in a mirror or a shop window.
- I want to stop overeating and ignoring my body's sign that I am full.
- I want to stop yelling at my husband/boyfriend/kids/pets...
- I don't want to watch three hours of TV every night.
- I don't want to break the promises I made to myself anymore.
- I want to stop smoking.

These are obviously examples again. Write down all the things you don't want anymore!

Even though you can only change YOURSELF and nobody else, it's nice to think about what you won't tolerate anymore. Just the decision alone is very powerful. Setting boundaries doesn't mean that you want to change the other person. You just make very clear what's okay for you and what's not. To set these boundaries, you first have to realize what bothers you. Now is the time to change this.

Just keep writing without thinking. Write about what you DON'T want anymore. I know this is weird if you are used to positive thinking. I'm all into that too, but sometimes it's just a relief to shout out LOUD what kind of shit is not working anymore. After that, we'll get very clear on what we want instead, and there you go, we're on the positive track again.

At work, I no longer want to get treated as if I had nothing to say. I'm not the assistant, so I don't want to make coffee anymore. I don't want this role any longer.

I don't want to get yelled at by ...... insert who yells at you. Your kids? Your spouse? Your boyfriend? Your friend? Your boss?
I no longer want my boss to comment on my looks.

Continue writing down what you don't want to tolerate anymore. How you want to get treated instead and what role you play in the situation are not our topics right now. Just state what you don't want anymore.

Are you done? Nothing left to let go of what you don't want anymore?

End your letter with something like this:
Thank you, dear full moon, for taking all this in and helping me to let it clear away alongside you as you get smaller and smaller. Thank you for your support and your beauty.

And now BURN it! What? Are you crazy? I can't make a fire in my house!

Yeah, a fire in the house is a bad idea, but maybe you have a balcony? With an empty flowerpot? Do you have a BBQ-grill? Or you even have a fireplace in your house?

If you are really into this ritual, and you have the chance to go outside and make a beautiful bonfire somewhere, you can throw this full moon letter into the flames, it's extra powerful! Just burn it, in any way possible. Watch the handwritten words vanish. Watch the limiting beliefs and thoughts, and everything you don't want anymore, turn to smoke and ashes. This is magic. This works. And even though you might think I'm crazy and this is a little too witchy for you, just go with this ritual. It's simple, and it's powerful. That's what I love most about this. So simple: Write, burn, feel the difference. Wohooooo!

In my Joy Mastermind Program, we'll do this on any full moon or on winter or summer solstice. I tell everyone to burn it, if possible, and ask them to post a video or a picture of the burning letter into our private Facebook group. Of course, the burning part is optional, and nobody has to do something they don't want to, but last time, every single gentleman and lady in the group posted a pic or video, and we commented and had so much fun. One of the guys told us, "I brought my daughter to bed and then told my wife, 'I have to burn something I wrote at the mastermind session this morning.' My wife asked, 'Burning what? Are you caught in some cult or what?'" So funny, as mostly it's the opposite way—that the men are thinking we are nuts for doing such witchy rituals. Well, the world is changing, and I love to be part of it. I love to spend my time with YOU here, now, talking about fire, and full moon and letters that get burned.

The full moon takes things you don't want anymore and becomes smaller and smaller with them. Fire lets things vanish. This is a powerful combination, and I think it's really not that important whether you believe this or if you're just playing along, because writing and burning letters is fun. If you're not able to burn your paper, rip it into a thousand pieces. Flushing the little paper bits down the toilet can be very satisfying, too—

though it's not as romantic as the fire, for sure. What I really want to stress is: Don't leave this list lying around at your place. You don't have to be all into energies and woo-woo, but this paper is loaded with "heavy" stuff. Get rid of it the same day, okay?

I know a lovely couple that does this journaling fire-ritual together every month. One mastermind-lady does this with her whole family. Maybe you want to get your partner and family on board, too? Maybe you live surrounded by nature, and making a fire in the woods is easy for you? Imagine how magical this experience is for you, but also for your children and hopefully for your partner. This kind of tradition will have a big influence and enables them to think of the things they don't want anymore, which is so valuable in life!

Wait, there is more! Only journaling about the things we don't want anymore is just half the fun. The full moon gets smaller with the things you don't want anymore, and THEN, the new moon is here. The new moon is the perfect day for journaling about your intentions for the month. What do you want to be-do-have in the next month? THIS letter to the new moon is like a wish list to Santa, but also, an action plan. You know what's coming up in the next month, and you can write down things like:

Dear New Moon

Thank you for being the symbol up in the sky. I can see you growing and getting bigger. Thank you for supporting my intentions of growing and becoming the person I want to be. Thank you for growing with me so I can grow into the following intentions during the next month:

- I'll stay calm and relaxed at the family gathering next weekend. (Maybe this is usually a day full of anxiety and stress. Set your own compass for your feelings and make this statement of staying cool and even enjoying the event.)
- I'll listen very closely when my little kid/partner/etc. talks to me, I'm present and really enjoy being with them/him/her.
- I'll charge my phone in the kitchen and read in bed instead of playing games.
- ....

I'm sure you get what I mean!

You can end the letter with something like:
Thank you for all this. Thank you for helping me grow in all these ways. Thank you for your support and for being my reminder!

If you don't like letter-writing, that's totally okay. We only do what we really like in our life anyway, right? Don't let anyone tell you how to do things, if you feel it in your gut, that you don't want to do it that way, do it YOUR way. Check in with your inner wisdom. You carry the whole wide Universe within you.

You are powerful!

This letter or list is not your big fat vision. This is a short term, really nice way to decide what you want to be aware of, what you want to achieve, and what you want to focus on. These intentions are powerful. Only write things down you'll be thrilled to achieve, become, and manifest, okay?

I like to keep this letter in my journal. But, if you enjoyed the burning ceremony, you can imagine how the flames and the smoke carry your words up to the moon and to the Universe. You can design your own moon ceremonies! Again: Do what feels good and fun!

Now you have a new tool in your hand to become aware of what you no longer want, can get rid of on a full moon night and how you can use the new moon magic to set your intentions of what you WANT. Nice!

Let's get even more practical. I talk about this next tool on the men's book side, too (not the moon ritual, though. They have to find that themselves on *our* side of the book. If you tell your man about it, or even better, you just do your moon magic, he might be curious and possibly join you. You decide!), but I'll use another example here. Take a peek there if you want to know more.

I learned this technique from Jens Corssen. He's a behavioral therapist, a psychologist, and a very awesome speaker and author. I can highly recommend his book, *The Way of the Self-Developer.* For eight hours, I had the honor of listening to this man at a live event over ten years ago. His energy is contagious, and his stories accompany me to this day. I bought his audiobook and listened to it repeatedly. There were no smartphones and no online-audiobooks available back then, but my luxurious 120GB iPod (heavy like a stone) was filled with my inspirational CDs. Do you listen to inspirational books while you do chores like laundry (thank God, that's Ken's job), cleaning the kitchen, tidying up, or preparing meals? I love it so much, I learn so much, and I can highly recommend it to you.

Jens Corssen's book is entirely about thinking and how your thoughts are super powerful and super important. Your thoughts determine how you react to ANY situation. You hear & see something, and your thoughts go wild. You judge, you evaluate, and then you decide what your reaction should be, right?

If you are able to control and choose your thoughts, you are fully in control of your reactions, and that's really cool. If someone calls you out on something you didn't do at all in the first place, you could:

1. Yell back
2. Call him or her whatever nice words you have in your vocabulary
3. Start crying
4. Get really quiet and sad
5. Breathe and count to ten
6. Totally ignore this person
7. Ask: Why are you saying this to me? Explain it to me!
8. Tell this person to stop, breathe deeply, and then you explain the situation from your point of view
9. Stand up, fold your arms and look very intimidating
10. Begin to laugh

Stupid example? You can take ANY situation in your life and check in with yourself: What do I think about this, why do I react like this, and what are my ten options now? At work, at home, with your friends, with your neighbors. You always have options, and you can always choose how you want to react.

Write down all the situations in your life, when you get or got angry (within seconds or where it builds up over weeks), pissed, sad, stranded, mad, helpless... just the situations you hate to be in, the situations in which you would like to disappear or punch everyone or... you know your life, write everything down!

Now for every situation, think of ten options on how you could react differently than you usually do. Include the ones you normally fall for, like getting really angry or getting really quiet... and then think of other options for the rest of the ten.

This might seem simple, but it's not. These situations occur all the time in your life; otherwise, you wouldn't have written them down. So, your "catalog" of reactions will be in your mind the next time it happens again. Maybe you can't implement your brilliant other options right away, but you're already more in thinking-mode than just reacting the same way as always. This will change things. This will have a huge influence on your life!

It's like a workout. You don't see results right away, but over time, you're building your thought- and reaction-muscle to how YOU WANT. You choose! Choosing is always so much more powerful than just reacting automatically, "because I just am that way." You are not directed by the circumstances. YOU are the boss of your thoughts and actions!

The good thing is that you have written down your vision already. You know what your dream life looks like, that's so good! Before we go and get there, I want to continue, step by step, with the decluttering of thoughts, behaviors, and situations that you are in NOW. Working through the ugly or sad or grinding side of life is not easy, but so worth it! Getting rid of what doesn't serve you anymore is very powerful, and in your future vision you are a powerful lady, right? Powerful, self-confident, fit, healthy, strong, free, loved. Let's get rid of everything that is not helping you become this super "shero" that is already inside you, waiting to get out!

Do you know Jesse Itzler? Surely you know his wife Sara Blakely, the inventor of Spanx, self-made billionaire and my big inspiration? I found Jesse through Sara's Instagram account, and you definitely should follow both of them. I love how he creates his life with personal challenges, like running hundred-mile races, how he spends time with his family and four kids, how independent he and Sara are in their relationship together, what a strong couple they are, AND how he treats his gang of friends. Check him out, you'll love him, I'm very sure!

Jesse has a really cool TED Talk (I'll post the link on the book-bonus page www.joyismycompass.com/bookbonus, but you'll find him on Google too!) where he speaks about the "happiness meter."

He says: Imagine you put your whole life into a gigantic mixer. You blend all the areas of your life. He calls them buckets: Family, Wellness, Business, Important Causes, Friends. I love the wheel of life better, but it's the same way of thinking your life through. So, you throw all of your life into this blender. What number would you rate your overall life between one and ten?

(You really have to watch his TED Talk!) Everyone wants a ten, right? But that's like "too much" "too perfect" because of this, that, and the other thing is not working/not yet fulfilled/sucks/...

Fill in the blanks! What made you back out from your initial ten? Catch these thoughts and write them down. Maybe you'll have a really big AHA–moment here?

Something like this:
- Yeah, it's my relationship with my man, we're always fighting, and it's exhausting.
- I just hate my job, I don't want to work there anymore, but I'm scared that I'll never find a job I like, so I'd rather stay in this shitty job!
- Hmmm, I just don't have enough money. I'm living paycheck to paycheck, and I buy things I can't afford with money I don't have.

What's on your list? Write it down.

Changing these things in your life and resolving them is the to-do list for your happiness. Easy? Not at all? You can do it! The first thing is awareness, and you clearly have that, now. Thank you, Jesse! I love this tool so much; I always use it in my coaching and in my Joy-Mastermind. You should hear them say, totally amazed, "Wow, that's it? That's what's missing for having a ten out of ten?"

I know you did a lot of work already with your personal wheel of life. But this trick concentrates EVERYTHING in your life into one blender, and the insight can be mind-blowing.
Look at your list of things that should change to make your life a ten out of ten.

Maybe again, it's the question: What is it that you DON'T want any more in your life? You already gained really helpful insights if you did the full moon exercise. If you haven't done the full moon exercise yet, think of the thoughts, behaviors, reactions, moods, habits, but also people, you want to get rid of. Getting rid of people? Yes, people who are only dragging you down, driving you crazy, criticizing you constantly, you name it. They don't deserve a place at your table.

It works exactly the same with habits. Habits that make you angry, moody, tired, sick, etc., don't deserve to get any time or energy from you. They have to GO! Of course, only if you want to. You can keep anyone and anything in your life because you choose to, even if you know that it's not good for you. You are completely free to decide!

Let's play it through with smoking. If you don't smoke, take something else you want to change that you always fail to follow through on:

"I tried to quit smoking, but it didn't work. I can't."

No way. You just don't want to quit smoking. That's all. If you own this and say, "Okay, right at the moment I don't want to quit. So, I smoke." That feels so much better than playing some sort of a victim, acting like you can't do anything.

"Do, or do not. There is no try."
~ Yoda

I literally know nothing about *Star Wars*, except for this Yoda quote that I love so freaking much!

Don't try to break your bad habits or try to stop doing things. Trying is losing already. Do it and stick with it. Or don't do it, and own it.

Breaking up with cigarettes is not as hard as breaking up with people, but you can look at it the same way. Oh wow, I had another evening with her, I feel so freaking tired, and she talked so much without asking me even once how my life is going...

Will you tell her that you don't have time for her next time she asks? No? Yes?

If you don't want to kick her out of your life, that's completely okay! But just knowing that it's okay to do it when the time is right, sets you in a different place of power. And who knows— maybe your relationship will shift and become a really good one.

I'm not at all thinking that you should kick every annoying person out of your life. Some annoying people we like very much and don't want to kick out, but you want them to CHANGE!

Bad news: You can't change anybody but YOURSELF.

Don't like hearing that?

I've told you this many times before but I love this fact: You only own YOUR thoughts, YOUR dreams, YOUR vision, YOUR action, YOUR mood. You are not responsible for anybody else but yourself. Isn't that a relief? You're not responsible for your man, you are not even responsible for your kids. They are whole human beings who want to live life their way.

You might say, "No no no, I have to tell them what to do, when to do it, and how to behave."

Really? You could start today to treat them as your partners in crime. SHOW them how to treat others, how to behave. For example, don't yell at little people that they should stop yelling. Try whispering or speaking in a very calm voice and show them how YOU do life.

How do you treat your belongings? Very carefully and respectfully? They, *for sure*, watch you ALL THE TIME. They watch how you treat their father or your husband, your

 DECLUTTERING ON THE INSIDE

boyfriend. That's how they learn about relationships and how to communicate.

This applies not only to children, but the adults in your life, too. This book is not a parenting book, for sure! You have a big influence on EVERYONE around you. How about your boyfriend, your husband, or the man you dream about? Do you show your spouse the respect and love you want to get from him? Do you treat him how you want to be treated? How did your relationships look, when you did the one-hundred-year-old-looking-back exercise? Are you doing things that way already, or is there loads of room for improvement?

Can we meet your future self for a minute? Try to imagine it, just for fun! You'll gain a ton of insights. Let's choose her to be you in ten years, okay? So, she's not yet one hundred years old, but still quite a bit older than you. She is the **best version** of yourself. She was very conscious of her decisions in the last decade! She did all these freaky exercises from this crazy Swiss woman and read a ton of other books and listened to inspiring podcasts, and she knew: This is MY life. I can decide how to spend every day and be how I choose to be. She decluttered her home and her life and took action BIG TIME to create the life of her dreams. The big fat vision was and is still clear!

Imagine your future self entering the coffee shop where we're meeting. Look at her! She looks so beautiful: Healthy, radiant, full of energy, strong, and just happy!

Her energy is contagious. You already feel somehow better just by looking at your future self. WOW! That's ME? In ten years? YES! This is you. Let's meet her and talk to her and learn ALL THE THINGS she did to get to the point in her life, where she obviously is rocking it in a big way!

Give her a big warm hug. Feel how trained and healthy her body is! She didn't do it overnight. She worked for this every single day. No, you don't have to become a gym person, if you hate it there. You design your life on your terms, remember. So, if she is so strong and healthy and radiates power, she did it YOUR way, of course.

Feel how much she loves you! She's your biggest fan. Your fan from the future. She knows exactly what you're going through. She knows all your fears and your dreams. She loves you just the way you are now. You don't have to change to get her approval.

She tells you how awesome you are, how big and small decisions will have a huge influence on you, and your life right in the next weeks and months. You will not be the same in even half a year. You are rocking it so wildly!

Imagine that she sits down with us. Oh, shall I leave? I don't want to disturb your conversation at all! Let me throw in some questions you could ask her, before I go, okay? It seems like an interview, but hey, you want to know all her secrets! Her moves! Her habits! Her self-care. It's super clear to you that this woman takes very good care of herself. You are amazed that this is YOU!

Read through these questions. The first answers in your mind and imagination are the answers of your future self, okay? These kinds of mind-boggling exercises are so helpful. You get your advice not from ME, but from YOUR future self. Of course you'll listen more to her. I get that, and I love that! She's your super shero. She's your role model. And that's exactly what I want her to be for you. SHE can help you achieve more in the next six months than anyone else in your life. Isn't that cool? An imaginary friend who happens to be your best version of your future self in ten years.

Yep, you don't have to tell anyone! Yes, this can be your secret weapon! Yes, this is crazy, but you don't care, right?

If you are ready to get even "crazier", do the future-self meditation that you can download on the book-bonus page www.joyismycompass.com/bookbonus.

During the meditation, you will meet your future self, as before, and be able to ask her questions. The helpful difference is that you are in a meditative state of mind, where your judging mind is "waiting in the corner" and not yelling mean comments all the time. That way, you can experience the whole scene with an openness, which is such a cool experience. I do this meditation with all my clients, and it's crazy what they tell me about what they "experienced" and saw, like a movie with clear pictures and super practical insights. On top of the advice you get from your future self, you FEEL her energy, and that can be life-changing (I know this word is so overused, but sometimes, it's just that!). You gain more motivation to change your life through this, more than with any other advice from anyone. So, did I convince you to do the meditation? YOU decide.

You can gain great insights by just answering the questions, which I still didn't give you. But now it's time to fully go into this scene of you and your powerful future self, sitting in this coffee shop, and talking about life:

How did you even start changing your situation?
If you were me right now, what would be your next important step?
I'm totally overwhelmed with making all these changes... I want to stay where I am, but hey, I see YOU, and I'm amazed... tell me how you did it!
What would you do in my situation with .... (insert challenge/issue/problem)?
Shall I keep in contact with.... (insert the person you are not so sure about still keeping in your life)?

Maybe you're curious, and maybe she'll answer. Maybe she doesn't want to spoil your experience and keeps some secrets to herself. But just ask, you'll get the answers or not.

Where do you live now?
Are you in a relationship? With whom?

If you are in love now and it's brilliant, or difficult, maybe you will hear her tell you that in ten years you're still together. Since your future self looks so damn great, she must have a blast with her man, yes? Isn't that soothing? Isn't that the greatest motivation to take care of your relationship in a very deliberate way? You can do this! Step by step. We'll get to this in the next chapter.

If you are single now and you're looking for an awesome man to rock your life with, you will surely hear that from her and how you found your soulmate. A really cool man, who is absolutely thrilled that he found YOU! Isn't that nice?!

If you are single now and you don't want to change anything about this situation because you love to be on your own, GREAT! I'm pretty sure that your future self will tell you stories about how amazing her life is, with or without a man in it.

Ask any question off the top of your head and think of the first answer that comes to mind. I told you, that's a lot easier in the meditation, so just TRY IT. It's fun and free, so you don't have any excuses.

She'll motivate you when you are down! She'll tell you, show you that everything will work out perfectly, even though it might seem impossible at the very moment. She's your wing woman, and if you want to have her in your life, just think of her as your invisible coach. You can have her by your side in any situation, and ask for help and advice. Remember the difficult situations and the ten options we discussed at the beginning of the chapter? She can help you in any stress-situation to find ten cool options, OR she just can tell you what to do, because she resolved such situations in the past, too.

So, if you're fighting with someone, remember your future self. Whisper to her in your mind, "What should I say or do right now?" You might be stunned at what enters your mind: "Walk away, this is not worth it!" or maybe you're fighting with your spouse, and you are so mad. She might whisper, "Now is the time to just go over and take him in your arms and hug him dearly!"

WHAT? Hug him? NOW? We're fighting!

I suggest making a deal with your future self and promise to take her advice without exception. How can she coach you if you don't listen? If you have the power to get new inputs like hugging your man in a fight instead of handling the situation like you always would, how freaking powerful is that? Just listen to the voice in your head. It's her, and you know her. She's doing really well, and you want to be like her, so it might be a really good idea to follow her advice.

If you think, "No way I'll EVER become that super shero," stop this limiting train of thought right in its tracks. Just ask your coach, AKA your future self, loads of questions in any moment of stress or insecurity. If you are building up this relationship with her, you just WON YOUR LIFE!

 Yes, it's all in your mind (and heart), and it doesn't hurt, and you can stop it anytime, but don't miss out on this. She can help you with the challenges you have to conquer to fetch a ten on the happiness meter. And quit smoking, if that's what you want to do. She's your wing woman. She's your coach. She's your inspiration! She's your motivation.

Do the meditation too, okay? Deal?

Thank you for spending all this time with me. Thank you for being open-minded (and maybe a little "crazy") enough to try these tools and exercises. You're doing it for you! You will see the changes rolling in, and these changes are going to be AWESOME!

The next chapter is all about self-care. You saw your future self. She's in such good shape, physically and mentally, she's doing the right things at the right time, and that's what we'll talk about. Self-care is not just spending time in spas getting a manicure and a pedicure. It's about taking care of your body and mind and soul DAILY in a very individual, personalized way that suits YOU and no one else.

Ready? Let's do this!

SELF-CARE

You Deserve to Be Taken Care Of

self-care
/ self-ˈker /
noun

The practice of taking action to preserve or improve one's own health.

o The practice of taking an active role in protecting one's own well-being and happiness, in particular during periods of stress.

I'd make this definition even bigger and add: The practice of taking the non-negotiable, leading role in improving one's own well-being and happiness, every single day.

Let's find out what YOU need to improve or preserve or take care of in your life so that you feel happy and healthy and strong and confident.

I have eight questions for you. Just answer them right away without overthinking, okay?

- Who do you trust most?
- With whom do you love to spend time the most?
- Who knows all your secrets?
- Who knows all your forbidden dreams?
- With whom can you discuss your Be-Do-Have list for hours?
- Who do you love wholeheartedly?
- Who is the most important person in your life?
- Who can you ask: What's my next step?

If you answered "my future self" for the last question, I love you even more than before!

So, how many times did you answer with "ME"? Zero? Eight out of eight?

Did you even consider yourself as an answer to these questions?

"But I sound like an egomaniac if I put in myself as an answer!" Really? I don't agree.

Of course you love to spend time with your friends or your man or your family, but you are with yourself from your first breath until your last. You spend every second of your living time with yourself, so, it would be really nice if you loved to be with yourself, trust yourself, and love yourself, right? It would be wonderful if you were aware of your power, and aware of how taking care of yourself is a really good thing. That way you would have more energy, you would feel better, you would be happier, and with all that you would have more to give! Your personal and business relationships would benefit because, hey, it's just nicer to work with a cheerful person than with a grumpy one. It's also more enjoyable to live with a woman who takes care of her own needs and doesn't expect her partner or others to fulfill her (untold) expectations.

Let's dig into this self-care topic in a really practical way. Self-care is something you DO every day.

Of course, you are customizing this to your own needs and your personal taste, okay?

We'll cruise through all the areas of your life and talk about how caring for yourself could look like for you. Shall we start with food this time? By "food" I mean "nutrition."

Nope, I won't call you out if you eat fast food. I'm the biggest believer that if you enjoy your food to the fullest, it's doing you good, whatever it is. This means that you need to get super clear on what you WANT to eat, and then, enJOY it without any guilt involved.

What I also love to focus on: How does your food make you feel?

Think of your car. You give your car fuel, and you don't put diesel in your tank if it needs gasoline. You check the oil frequently and just take good care of your (beloved) vehicle. And if it's worn down, old, and doesn't work anymore, you buy a new one.

The thing is, you've only got one body. Buying a new one is not possible, and getting spare parts is rather difficult so let's take great care of your wonderful body.

Remember how your future self looked so confident, radiant, fit, and healthy? She put in the work to feel that way, and she cares a lot about her own dreams and feelings. Her dream (which is your dream, now) was to get in shape and feel the power of healthy, yummy nutrition every day and she did just that! Because the beauty standards of our society don't interest her.

Shall we switch to your perspective? *You* decide what your daily self-care looks like now, and in the future, you'll see the results. No quick, short-term results—deeply rooted, good feelings in your body and mind that will show in your energy level and your overall health. Let your future self help you with that!

Food. Soul and Body Fuel.

For one semester, I taught food engineers about nutrition at the Zürich University of Applied Sciences. The schoolmaster asked me to create a new curriculum to inspire and motivate these students about this topic. I began my research and decided soon after that it just was not possible for me to choose out of all the topics what was important and tell them, "THIS is the truth, memorize it and then pass a test." During my five years at university studying food science, the facts we were taught in nutrition changed 180 degrees, two times. First, fat was bad, but carbohydrates were good. All these light- and low-fat products sprung up like mushrooms in the supermarkets. Later, carbohydrates became the EVIL thing to eat. Low carb, keto diet, blah blah blah!

I'm a big fan of all these hypes...NOT!

As for my students, I decided to challenge them. I ordered thirty books on Amazon: *The Truth About Carbohydrates*, *Why Carbs*

Are BEST for Your Body, *Eat Only Fat, and You'll Get Slim*, and so on. I'm making these titles up, but that's the kinds of books I chose, all kinds of titles that totally disagreed with each other. There were books about vegan, keto, Atkins, low fat, low carb. Each student read one book and held a presentation about the topic at the end of the semester. The bottom line of ALL these books is MY food philosophy: YOU have to find out what is best for you. No expert, no guru, no one but YOU can decide what's good for you.

Oh cool, so I can drink six big bottles of soda every day and eat doughnuts for dinner?
Of course, you can! You can do whatever you want. No one can force you to eat broccoli, or whatever it is you hate!

It's your choice, what you eat and drink. Good for you, right?! And who is helping you decide? I know her, she's so rad. She's the coolest. You know her! She's working for free, and she adores you and wants only the best for you. If you didn't see your future self smiling at you as you were reading my description, you'd have to reread the last chapter.

Put her into your head and heart. Discuss with her what you should choose to eat and drink, and after you've decided, you had better enjoy these doughnuts to the fullest and drink these sodas with a smile. Oh, no, she will not let you eat this kind of food? Poor you? Are you forced into more healthy choices? I bet you and your future self will have a blast while finding out what you want to eat today, tomorrow, and every day.

Let's do some journaling, shall we?

Write a list of ALL your favorite dishes, products, and treats. Just EVERYTHING you love to eat! Don't forget your childhood favorites! Maybe it was your grandpa's lasagna?

How many times did you eat food you love last week? Last month? You can write these numbers behind the items on your list. Maybe you'll see that you love Thai-curry so much, but you didn't eat it once last month.

Go through your list together with your future self and discuss the different meals and treats. Which ones should you reserve for special occasions? Which ones do you want to push to the top ten? What could you add to the list, without making any compromises about liking the food you eat? What could you try that you've never tried before?

If you're done with your list, you can think about last week: Monday through Sunday. Write down everything, every meal, and snack you ate, and all the drinks you had. Think about how every single item made you feel, and you'll gain great insights again about what's good for your body.

You already decided on the food you want to eat in the future, correct? What I think is at least equally important as WHAT you eat, is HOW you eat.

Eat and drink "with full appreciation," and I guarantee that you'll find a healthy balance between all the treats and your well-balanced meals. Try to enjoy every bite. Listen to your body. If you're full, don't eat another plate. Start communicating with your body more and more, and don't let your future self off the hook. She's your wing woman. She can tell you what she would choose to eat in this red-hot minute, and then, YOU decide if you want to listen or not.

If you are in a relationship, and your man is not eating what YOU want him to eat, maybe it's time to let this stress go? I know we women can feel responsible for so many other people. For the man, the kids, the dog, the grandma... I invite you to stop that.

"Are you crazy? I AM RESPONSIBLE for all these people and pets, and I'm always worried that they don't get the right nutrients, the right amount, and only eat healthy..." Is that you?

You are only responsible for yourself. By taking care of yourself, you are providing the greatest gift to your loved ones. You, being full of energy is your responsibility.

That's easier said than done, I know... but think about this fact.

How can you find more time for your self-care?

It's not selfish to tell your partner to take care of "everything" and go away for a weekend.

It's not egoistic if you have somebody taking care of your "home-business", and you go for a bike ride, lay in the grass, and read a book.

It's the BEST THING for you to make yourself a priority. If you are clear about how you want to create this sacred time for yourself, whether it's daily or weekly or (no, monthly is not enough) once in a while, you'll organize it. It's as important as a business meeting. It's as important as a non-negotiable business trip.

I need lots of time for myself. Becoming a parent was my biggest challenge. I thought, "Now, I'm glued to this tiny little human forever, and I'll never ever be able to go wherever I want anymore." I had serious postpartum depression. I didn't ask for help. I felt lost and left alone, even though my husband was a champion in doing ALL the housekeeping and even the cooking. This breastfeeding game was overwhelming for me, even though I had wanted to do it. But with time, it worked out great. It became easier with time and practice, and finally, my husband and I made crystal clear agreements about who is responsible for what and when. In my eyes, that's THE trick for parents or partners without kids to have a great relationship and not fight over daily things. If you know what YOUR job is, you do your job as soon as it fits your schedule. If you know that this and that is your partner's or kid's job, you just let them do their job when they think it's time for doing it.

No, you are not responsible for controlling them. It's an agreement, and it counts. Just trust them. Maybe it annoys you that they do it differently than you would do. Maybe they are too slow in your eyes. Not your business. Your business is to count on them without pushing your standards on them. I'm very lucky that my husband does the laundry and folds our clothes a hundred times more beautifully than I can. He cooks, and the kitchen is as clean as an operating room. When I cook, it looks like a tornado just hit. Our meals are equally tasty, though.

In 2015, we spent five weeks in Japan, traveling and spending lots of time in my father-in-law's beautiful new house in Takatsuki near Osaka. I was longing for ME-time. Time without my husband, without my kid, without ANYBODY! I just wanted to stay home in my pajamas and just BE. My husband asked me in great disbelief: "You want to waste a full day just staying at home? Okay, I'm going shopping for some fishing gear. Bye, bye!"

Ha! And here I was again with my stubborn five-year-old, who needs to learn to write the ABCs correctly and not in her way... We were fighting the whole day, and I was exhausted again. Exhausted, even though I should have been so happy to be in my favorite country, Japan, not working, just happy traveling, enjoying family time, right!?

That evening I had a big girl tantrum and called everybody in the room names, and yelling that TOMORROW I'LL GO WHERE I WANT, AND I DON'T WANT ANY COMPANY, AND JUST LEAVE ME ALOOOOOONE!

The next day, I went to a temple in the mountains above Kyoto. I was the only foreigner on the bus, which is something I love to be. I feel so deeply connected to Japan and its people. I enjoyed the loneliness and the quietness while riding upward for an hour and a half through a quiet green valley. Finally, I found where my favorite ojizo-san, little statues made of stone, are situated! I was so excited to see them in real life. The first time I saw a picture of the one that I fell in love with immediately, was on a menu of a fancy hotel in Munich, Germany. There I decided that I would like to visit this ojizo-san in person one day. It was totally and absolutely magical. I sat in this temple garden in front of these figurines for hours. Just being still and looking at them made me so happy and calm. All of a sudden, it felt like the ojizo-san was sending a message to me: "Go yukkuri tanoshinde kudasai" (Take it slowly and enjoy). Wherever this sentence came from, it touched my heart and soul. A poster of this ojizo-san is in my office and reminds me every day to take it easy, take time for myself, and enJOY my life. I realized that I am responsible for creating my much-needed me-time in every situation. During work-time and mama-time, at home, or on our vacations. This I promised myself, up there in the mountains of Kyoto. Taking time just for myself is not selfish and not egotistic. It's a necessity!

But hey, we don't need fancy trips to Japanese temples to carve out some ME-time! It can be half an hour in the afternoon, it can be a cup of tea or a week away. It doesn't matter. What matters most is your mindset. Let go of all the responsibilities and trust that your partner, your friend, your whoever, will do a great job, and he or she will do it their own way. You don't have to check-in and feel responsible from afar. Just enjoy YOUR time! This is important for any time frame.

In the chapter "Habits", I'll introduce you to my morning-magic routine that saves me, fills me up with energy, and generates my good mood every day. Actually, we are still on the food topic. But this insertion was so important because of your guilty feeling of being responsible for everybody around you.

Could you also let go of the thought that you have to make your husband drink green smoothies? Could you let go of the fights over broccoli or other healthy food nobody likes? If you don't fight over these topics, good for you! I know so many families and couples who argue over food, and I think that's such a disadvantage for everybody involved and has a huge impact on our kids' future choices as soon as they can decide on their own what to eat and how much. I vowed to myself to have harmonious meals with my family and NOT fight over food even before I had a kid, and I tell you, that was a good choice. I eat vegan, lots of veggies, and make myself the yummiest food ever. Ken loves meat and fried stuff, and veggies and salad is just a minor matter. Mika ate everything until she was a one-year-old. Since then, she has become the pickiest eater, and thank God, she still likes fruits, but veggies are like poison to her. Inedible. At first, she was in daycare, and now she eats in school two times a week, but she doesn't like lunch: She just refuses to eat lunch and waits, without any complaints, until snack time and eats all the fruits. Fighting with her or with Ken would break ME, nobody else.

So, maybe by hearing these little snippets out of our life, it can help you to make your own vow to eat what's good for YOU.

My last wisdom on this topic: Let everybody eat as much or as little as they want from an early age. Listening to our bodies is so important. All the kids who have to take another bite or eat everything on their plate, they unlearn to listen to their bodies.

Okay, I'm finished preaching now. Thank you for listening.

If you want more wisdom on food, and even cooking classes to make things from scratch without a recipe, please check the men's side of the book. (Page 103)

Just make your food, your fuel, the gas for your body a priority!

You can do as many sports as you want, but your body's base is earned in the kitchen. They say seventy-five percent is what you eat and only twenty-five percent is how you move your body!

So, we tackled the seventy-five percent in this chapter. Just eat the best things you can find and ditch the crap. If you love sweets and junk food, I suggest you eat it on rare occasions. Otherwise, concentrate on fresh and made-from-scratch food. Oh, you're not up to that? No problem. You decide! Nobody demands accountability of you. As I told you in the beginning: Eating super unhealthy food with lots of pleasure and with a huge smile on your face is much better for your body than shoveling it in your mouth with loads of guilt and shame. Our mind is powerful. You can think it's healthy and that it makes you happy, and that becomes true. Cool, right? Do it your way, and love your food and your body with all your heart.

Let's go to movement, shall we?

Move Your Vehicle

Are you a typical couch potato? Super sporty? Well trained? Do you go to the gym daily? You do loads of workouts per week? Have you not once in your lifetime done any sports at all?

I don't know what shape you are in, obviously. I don't know what your starting point is, but I know for sure that EVERYTHING is possible. I'm sure you've seen the amazing videos where people lose two hundred pounds in two years (no quick things, please!) and how they just decided to change, and so they did? I know that's easier said than done, but it's doable.

> **ANY fitness goal is a good one, and hey, you saw your future self. She's in such great shape. So, ask her, "What did you do?"**

Think of the kind of movement you really like. Is it hiking? Walking? Swimming? Yoga? Don't judge yoga if you haven't tried it. I train with my YouTube-personal trainer, Yoga with Adriene. She comes over to my home with a click, for free. I love her, but there are a TON of different online trainers out there. Try it! Yoga is good for your mind and body and for any level of fitness or flexibility.

You think yoga is from the devil? Okay, okay... but why not challenge yourself and do yoga for a week or a month and ditch it after that, knowing that it really is from hell? Right now, you just don't know, right?

Running? Now THAT'S from hell, in my opinion. But hey, all you need is sneakers, and off you go. Try running for some minutes and walking for some minutes until you can run longer distances. If you want to get inspired to run, follow Jesse Itzler, the guy who talks about the happiness meter. He's so much into running that I sometimes almost get inspired, for a second, to try this stupid sport again. Just for a second, though...

You don't need a list of all the sports you could start doing. Just choose something you like, which is FUN! Why should you do something you don't like? By doing the sport you like, you'll get more and more in shape, and hey, you have a personal coach who's looking so damn good: Your future self. Choose her age and dial in to talk to her. Let her tell you what you should change - do - start. Martial arts? Zumba? Water gymnastics? You're laughing at that, but your joints will love you for dropping some pounds in the water.

Just shake up the cells of your body and DO SOMETHING... or do nothing with a smile, that's okay, too. Your choice. If you think eating healthy AND doing sports is too much, then choose healthy eating first. Balanced food has way more impact on your body than eating trash and doing some sports. DEAL?

Self-Care in Relationships

Is this going places you don't want to think about? Stay with me! Relationships can be the most beautiful thing in your life or the most devastating, and everything in between.

I don't want to go into psychology. I want to ask you again: What do you want in your relationships? How do you want to be treated? How do you want to treat others? What do you want to tell your loved ones, but never have up to now, because you were scared to do so? Maybe you think: "I'm not good at communicating, so I better say nothing?"

Can we please talk to your future self again for a minute? She figured out the way she wants to interact, communicate, and show love, appreciation, and affection to the people around her. She knows her boundaries. She says what she needs in a relationship. She knows what she wants in a relationship. She made it very clear what a no-go is for her. The rules in relationships are always a two-way thing. But first, you have to know what's important to YOU.

Journal it out! Write down everything you wish for in your relationships. A wish list for every important relationship you have. With your spouse, with your kid(s), with your neighbors, with your boss, with... Ah, you don't have a spouse? Well, you know what? The BEST way to pull the best man into your life is by writing down what you wish for. How is he, how are you with him? Write it down in the present tense, as if you would thank someone for your brilliant relationship, as if it were already reality.

Thank you for my wonderful man; he is so cool and kind. He knows what he wants and knows his own dreams. He is so self-confident that he doesn't care at all about the manly expectations of society. He is such a great house husband and is not too cool for that. For him, it's natural. It's so easy to be with him. We just love each other as we are. Nobody needs to change anybody. I know I don't have to take care of him or heal him. He takes responsibility for his own shit. I take responsibility for mine, and together we are a dream team. Thank you that I have such a light and fun relationship with him and that it feels so good! We are a team. He's my gang. He accepts my friends. I can go out without him; he can go out without me. We trust each other. That's so cool. And totally stress-free. Thank you for my man, he's just pure gold!

Is that too much to ask for? I don't think so. Is this not at all your personal dream of a romantic relationship? Write YOUR version, way to go! Think it through. Dream of your perfect partner.

Maybe you want the traditional thing: A strong guy who protects his little lady. Hmmm... are you sure? You can feel protected when YOU own YOUR own life. You can feel protected with and without a man, because you are a strong, powerful woman who knows what she wants! I prefer equality, seeing things eye to eye. I prefer to support each other out of strength, not weakness. I don't think men and women have to be the same, we are different anyway, but I believe in only being responsible for yourself. What he does is his business. I believe in trust. I believe in supporting each other's dreams. I believe in being kind to each other. I believe in surprising your man, having fun, celebrating life, feeling good, and having a damn good time together!

This applies to any relationship. I believe in having fun at work with your team or with your boss. No, life is not always a bowl of cherries, but why not bring a little lightness in the daily grind? Surprise your work colleagues with a fun or kind sticky note? With coffee?

Why not try talking to a homeless woman and buying her some nice food? This woman will love you for respecting her as a human being because they don't often have the chance to talk to somebody just in a normal, genuine way.

Relationships are everywhere, and YOU decide how to show up for yourself and others around you. But you have to know what you want. And as you are a journaling pro by now, you are writing down all of your thoughts on relationships, and I tell you, your relationships will change for the better!

"Is this self-care, Ronja?" I think YES! By knowing what you want and communicating that you are fully responsible for YOU and nobody else, that's powerful!

It's about being aware of who you are, how you show up, and how you treat your people. You decide. Decide wisely. You'll feel good for sure. And hey, if your relationships feel bad, if your personal rules are violated, or dismissed, you have to speak up. If the other person listens, you can discuss how you want to handle things together. If the other side won't listen to your requests, maybe that person is somebody to get rid of...? I know that sounds harsh, but there are people out there who are just your match. It feels easy, good, and in tune to spend time with them, and they appreciate you for who you are. You don't have to play a role. But people who always make you feel bad don't deserve to spend time with you!

I know... if that's your mom, your dad or at worst, your husband, you've got some work to do. Setting boundaries with your parents is not easy, but you can do it! If you feel bad being together with your partner, I want to encourage you to ask yourself: "Do I still love him? Do I still respect him? Can I think of our wedding day, when everything was so great? Do I want to figure things out with him together? Is he willing to figure this relationship out?" If yes, GO for it! Go to a counselor, or talk everything through with a friend who can help you two focus and not fight. But hey, sometimes it's just not the right person.

No, I don't want to encourage you to break up with your man. What I want is for you to have a really great, fulfilling, easy-going relationship where you feel seen, heard, respected, and supported. And I'm very, very, *very* sure that this is what your husband or boyfriend wants, too. The problem is that we often expect the other person to take care of our happiness. That's the wrong idea. You have to take care of your own feelings, your mood, your wellness, your energy. That way, your man is free of the duty to make you happy. And yes, this applies to him, too. Imagine how AWESOME that would feel. You could tell each other what you need, what you expect, what you would love to experience and do together. No guessing. Just clear and normal talking. No bitching or yelling. Just doing kind and fun and supportive things for each other. You can, because you took care of yourself first. You have the energy and the freedom to be nice to him. You don't expect him to make you happy. You are already happy.

"Aaaah, Ronja, this is soooo much to do and consider and change!"

You can do it! I totally believe in you! Don't rush, take one step at the time. Find out what you LOVE to do, what makes you happy, what you need to feel fit, healthy, energized, and creative. What you want to do in your free time. What you want to do for a living.

Decide how you want to show up on the stage of life. You don't need anyone else but YOU to change your world. And I'm sure, if you can remember the love and happiness you felt at your wedding day, you can fix your relationship because you fix yourself first. Talk with your man. He has the same kinds of fears and challenges, but if you just yell and fight with each other, nothing's going to change.

If you have a fantastic relationship already, this will maybe help a friend of yours who needs to hear this. Tell him or her what I told you, and his or her world will change! Better yet, give him or her this book after you're done reading it.

So. With each category of self-care, it's basically the same but a little different. It breaks down to: WHAT is it that you want? Get really clear about this on every spoke of your wheel of life. Money, travel, adventures... find out what you want and how to handle it and then go and DO it! Meet your future self, who is living this plan day by day, and achieved everything that you dream of. Get her advice. Get her support. And then, step by step, change yourself into the best future version you can imagine. Wow... how does that sound? I'm so freaking proud of you! This is the deal of YOUR LIFE! This is powerful!

So, let's make things happen. Now that you know what you want and thought things through, now we need ACTION!

HABITS

Good Habits Bring You Joy

When I was about ten, my father had extreme lower back pain, lumbago. He wasn't able to move for three days without having enormous pain. I still see him suffering, and at the time, I was thinking: "Oh no, my strong daddy is so weak in bed." A physiotherapist came to our house every day to train with him, and she gave my father a lecture on the importance of fitness. She gave him exercises for his back and whole body to do daily. And he did. Every single freaking morning, he still does these exercises, plus five minutes on the home trainer going full speed. This takes him about fifteen minutes plus a shower afterwards. He's eighty-one years old now, and fit as a fiddle. Every year before New Year's Eve, he walks for more than two hours to our mountain cabin with a backpack, step by step, without a hurry. He's up there first, because the rest of us are busy with taking care of the kids who need breaks to drink tea or rest, or if someone has to pee. He just walks, and arrives totally in Zen mode.

Would he be so fit if he wouldn't invest these fifteen minutes for his daily workout? Nope!

Are fifteen minutes per day an exhausting amount of time to invest in your health and fitness? Nope!

It's an easy thing to define good little habits for yourself to do daily, weekly, or monthly. The hard thing is to stick with them. My father has been doing these exercises for thirty-three years now. That's over twelve thousand times! Crazy, right? But the result is just too cool!

So, how about asking your future self? "Not AGAIN?!" Hey, if this cool healthy, fit and radiant lady (not my dad, YOUR future self) is not your role model, you are missing out!

You can meet your future self wherever you want in your mind and ask her, "What do you do on a daily, weekly, or monthly basis? What kind of habits are non-negotiable for you? How did

you get into such good shape, and how are you maintaining it?"
It's all about habits, like my father's. If the ideas don't pop in
your head easily, do my second future-self meditation in the
book-bonus section www.joyismycompass.com/bookbonus or
ask yourself, "Well she's in such great shape, she must do some
kind of sport. Which kind? What sport did I always want to try?"
You did this work already in the previous chapters, but now it's
GAME TIME! You decide when, where, what, and with whom.
You decide on your new habits you want to install.

You have to do it YOUR way!

Is that too lame? Not enough of a challenge? Well... I think it's
nice to just start and build from there. I'm super bad at habits
like doing sports, but I definitely feel better when I stick to it.
When I talk myself out of doing yoga or a workout in the
morning, I have back pain or headaches and tension in my neck
and shoulders. My body telling me to just DO the workout and
take care of myself. But hey, I'm not perfect, and I'm hanging in
here together with you.

It's not only sports habits that are the hardest for me. I also want
to integrate other daily habits, like:

- Journaling – at least 750 words per day. (Check
  750words.com!)
- Meditate – at least fifteen minutes of going deep and

getting all the cool answers for the day, new ideas, and support from within (yes, my future self is a regular guest at this meeting)

- EFT - Emotional Freedom Technique (Meet my guy, Brad Yates, on YouTube. He's the best, and has a video for any topic of your life. What is EFT? Just try it. It's free and weird, and you better make sure that your neighbors don't see you doing this. Ken, my husband makes fun of me when I tap. But guess what? I don't care. This technique is life-changing in getting rid of old limiting beliefs, fears, and other worries you never ever told anybody about.)

Write down all the habits you want to do. Write them ALL down! You have no idea what kind of habits shaped your future self? Dive into your vision, into your dreams, and look around: What kind of daily activities made this happen?

Bo Eason wrote a book with the title: *There's No Plan B for Your A-Game*. I had the big honor of attending Bo and Dawn Eason's live event "Personal Story Power" in La Jolla, California, in May 2019. Bo teaches to write down a declaration for your life's dream. He asks you: What do you want to be the BEST at in the whole wide world? Whether you want to be the best dancer, the best writer, or the best boss, he breaks it down to sixty-six-day challenges. You make a decision to focus on a habit or a habit stack for sixty-six days. He says that after sixty-six days of sticking to your new habit, it's easier for you to DO your habit than NOT doing it. What is "habit stacking"? That's a term from another great book: *Atomic Habits* by James Clear. He teaches how you can combine habits until you can't resist doing the second habit right after the first because you are so used to it, and you wired your brain that way.

Bo says sixty-six days, others say it takes twenty-one days, or thirty days to make a new habit stick. Whatever goal you are setting for yourself, whatever challenge you're committing yourself to, START IT! And then just DO it, every single day! Will you fail? Of course! Is that super bad? Not at all. Just get back into the game the next day.

In the men's part of the book, I tell the guys about the 75 Hard Challenge by Andy Frisella. Check it out if you are interested. There, you have a ton of habits to do every day for 75 days in a row. If you fail, you just start over again.

I personally don't like too many rules, but I like to use trackers. In the Joy Academy, we always use trackers. You can either use one of the various templates from the book-bonus page www.joyismycompass.com/bookbonus, or can you design your own. One of the wonder women in my mastermind drew all the tasks on a whiteboard. This board stares at her in her bathroom and wants to get colored in. Choose what you love to use as a support system.

Just fill in the habits you want to do, and off you go! This is the most boring design, so go and check out the other ones on the bonus page, or go to Pinterest or google " journal tracker." You'll be blown away by the beautiful trackers you'll find.

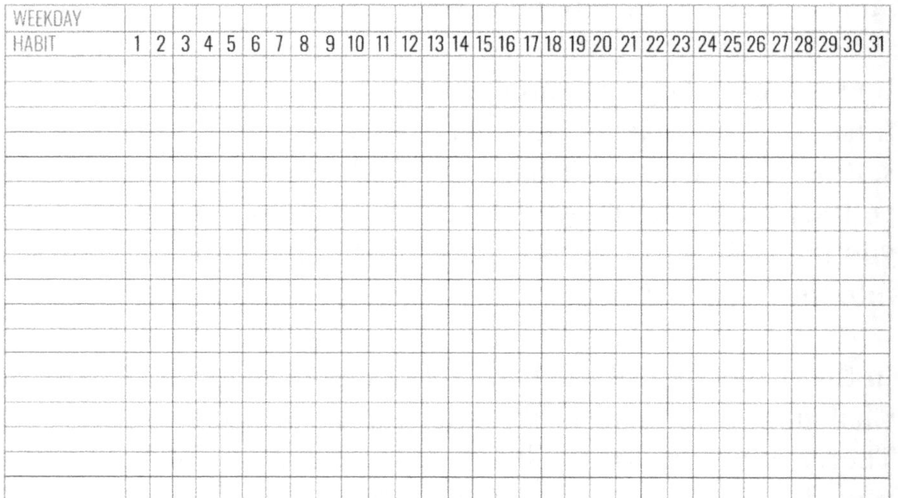

What should I commit too? Ask your future self! What does she do?

My personal list for my habits that have the "bestest" and the greatest and most wonderful impact on my mind and body are:

- **Some sort of sports**
  Yoga is my first choice, but a sweaty workout in the morning in my living room is a good way to start the day. I like to earn the morning shower, even though I hate sports.
- **Drink lots of water or herbal tea**

I quit drinking sugary drinks a long time ago. My goal is 3 liters/0.79 gallons per day.

- **Eat yummy AND healthy**
My food is so good. I chose to go vegan because I heard the screaming cows when I was passing the slaughterhouse in Zurich. That was the point where I finally decided to go vegan. It's healthy, and it's yummy, too!

- **Journaling**
Journal free flow or affirmations, a good old Be-Do-Have list, an ideal day, or just some words.

- **Meditate**
Mostly, I do a freestyle guided meditation in my head. I have recorded so many that I just go and see what comes up. I have some up my sleeve for you, free to use and choose from: www.joyismycompass.com/bookbonus.

- **Reading/Learning**
Before bed or during the day. I love online courses on all possible topics, and I love audiobooks.

- **EFT**
That's one of my favorites, as I told you. Check out Brad Yates on YouTube.

- **No phone in my bedroom**
I regularly cheat on this one, stupid me. I'm a social media addict, and I should know better to just leave my device in the living room.

- **Seven to Eight hours of sleep**
When that's not possible, I often take a nap in the

afternoon, like a grandma. I love my power naps of thirty-three minutes.

- **Gratitude practice before falling asleep**
  I don't journal what I'm grateful for at the end of the day, but this would be super powerful! I just go through the day in my thoughts and say thank you for all the good and cool things that happened.

The ones I REALLY have to put some effort into doing daily are: Exercising, meditating, journaling, EFT, no phone in the bedroom, and getting enough sleep. The ones which are totally installed, non-negotiable, and as normal as brushing my teeth are food, water, reading, and gratitude.

Now it's your turn! What do you want to change? How hard do you want to challenge yourself?

- Say no when you mean no?
- Stop watching TV for four hours a day?
- Get fit for hiking up a certain mountain?
- Be kind to your man every day?
- Stop yelling at your kids every morning? (What do you need to actually do this? More time? Okay, so get up earlier. Oh, and exercise in the morning for your own energy! If you take care of yourself first, caring for others is so much easier!)
- Stop moaning all day long?

- Be present in conversations?
- No phone at the dinner table?
- Eat your food with full presence and no distraction, like TV or phone?
- Go for a run in the neighborhood after work?

I'm not telling you what to do. YOU decide! And you really have to want to do it, otherwise, it's for nothing. Whatever habit you want to start from scratch, know that it's hard. It sucks. But the rewards will be so good!

Talk to your future self in your head. See her teasing you, hear her voice, and see her annoyingly fit with a strong and healthy body. See her smile and feel her contagious energy. Can you convince yourself that becoming HER is possible?

Just begin. You don't have to start with the perfect set of habits. Just start, and adjust as you go. Print out that tracker, fill in the habits, and the day you did it (daily, of course, right?) and color in the according square. That's all.

What helps to stick to it:
- Get an accountability partner
- Celebrate every week that you're still doing it
- Enjoy the coloring of the fields like a proud little girl
- Have your future self in your mind. She's your cheerleader!

If you want to know more about managing habits and why they are so super-powerful, read the book I told you about already: *Atomic Habits* by James Clear. This is such an amazing book, and he talks you into creating your habit stacks and how you should make your bad habits really annoyingly difficult—like putting your TV in a closet or always taking the batteries out of your remote and hiding them somewhere stupid. On the other hand, make your good habits really easy. Put your kettlebell and sports mat out in front of your bed so that you are reminded immediately when you get up!

Now HAVE FUN! You're doing this for YOU! You'll feel better, full of energy, and you'll gain strength. You will sleep better, and your mood will be elevated. The struggle of beginning to change is so worth it!

I can't wait to hear all your wins and aha-moments you've had. You are a super shero, and your "super shero future self" is helping you improve every day so you enjoy that your heart is beating. You are ALIVE and have choices!

CREATE JOY

You Rock!

We've made it to the last chapter! You've thought through your big fat vision, decluttered your home like a champ, decluttered your beliefs and old wounds. You've decided what your self-care should look like and put daily, weekly, or monthly habits into practice. HOW COOL IS THAT?

Now we're going to throw some icing on this cake. Some fun, joy, and other treats that bring a big smile to your face. This is as personal as all the other things we've discussed! What's fun for you doesn't have to be fun for your friends, husband, boyfriend, or future boyfriend. But guess what? You're again focusing on

YOU, and you'll have the most benefit out of this.

What brings you joy?

- A clean, shiny car?
- Dashing down a powdery mountain with your snowboard?
- Watching a game show?
- Singing country songs around a campfire with your guitar in your lap?
- Going for a walk with your dog?
- Your bulletproof coffee?

You see…? The examples couldn't be more different. That's why you have to write this list on your own. Write down one hundred things that bring you joy.

"One hundred? Are you insane?"

You know by now that I'm a crazy woman, so, just do it!
Ten is too easy. Twenty is easy, too… but one hundred… that's when you really have to think of all the BIG and little things that bring a smile to your face!

Go for it! One hundred things. NOW!

1.

2.

3.

4.

5.

6.

7.

8.

9.

10.

11.

12.

13.

14.

15.

16.

17.

18.

19.

20.

21.

22.

23.

24.

25.

26.

27.

28.

29.

30.

31.

32.

33.

34.

35.

36.

37.

38.

39.

40.

41.

42.

43.

44.

45.

46.

47.

48.

49.

50.

51.

52.

53.

54.

55.

56.

57.

58.

59.

60.

61.

62.

63.

64.

65.

66.

67.

68.

69.

70.

71.

72.

73.

74.

75.

76.

77.

78.

79.

80.

81.

82.

83.

84.

85.

86.

87.

88.

89.

90.

91.

92.

93.

94.

95.

96.

97.

98.

99.

100.

Write your list directly into this book. Yes, everyone who will read this book after you will be able to see it, and will be so inspired! My list is at least three hundred items long and growing daily. This brings you joy only by reading and writing it, and now it gets even better: This is your to-do list for every day.

Do as many things on this list as possible. I always say to do at least three! You are worth the effort, right? More joy brings more fun. A fun and joyful person is cooler to be around. With good energy around you, you attract success, the greatest friends, and the nicest man. You are relaxed, and as you take the best care of yourself, you have no expectations of your surroundings that they take care of you. You are FREE! So absolutely free! You don't have to please anyone but yourself. You exercised in the morning already. You enjoy your bulletproof coffee at home as much as a weekend of heli-skiing. You feel good. You choose to feel good.

Is that still too much for you to read? Do you feel uncomfortable? You don't want to be the good-mood woman in your team, in your family, in your neighborhood? You choose. AGAIN, you choose who you want to be. You can enjoy your good feelings, because you take such good care of yourself and have all these amazing habits, quietly and secretly. I tell you, it'll shine through. People will recognize the difference, and you will become a role model for many people around you, without even knowing it.

So now, as you are in such a good mood and state, let's do some fun stuff for others. I can tell you that your man will be THRILLED if you go all-in to bring fun and joy in his life, too. He knows that he's responsible for his own joy and wellbeing, but your actions are just extra treats in the day. These things work for kids, grandparents, roommates, whomever you live with. It even works for yourself!

Some of the things on this list may be perceived as super romantic, but you can give them any title you want, and, of course, you know your man and your family best. Just try to earn the smiles and happy faces:

- Write/draw nice little sticky notes, and place them into lunchboxes, in the fridge, on the door, in your purse.
- Buy the favorite drink/treat/fruit/juice and hide it somewhere with a little treasure hunt (Arrows are always so, so cool… for kids AND grownups!
- Buy flowers. Just because. Maybe you'll have them delivered with a card? Who is sending you flowers? Oh, right! It's me! I've never gotten flowers from my husband. In the seventeen years living with him in Zurich, I once got gorgeous roses, but he got them for free at work! Well, no matter. I buy my own flowers! (But I would love to get some for sure!) I told your man on the other side of the book to buy you flowers. Receive them with a big thank you. And if you don't get any, you just buy them yourself.

- Smuggle a little gift in his bag, in the schoolbag, or in the briefcase.
- Do their chore—of your kids, or the ones of your roommate or grandma! It's just so nice if you come home and hear: Oh, that's already done! I highly recommend that you have a plan in your home about who works on what, which things are just THIS person's job, and how you organize the whole cooking-dirty-dishes-never-ending-circle. If you live alone, you can learn for your future. When everybody has their jobs, it's possible to do this job for them and surprise them. You already heard that my husband is the laundry-boss in our house. If I'm working from home, and I'm REALLY nice, I sometimes wash a load of laundry and hang it up. I get bonus points if the sun is shining, and the laundry is hanging to dry in the sunshine! My job is to wake up our girl every morning and bring her to bed nearly every night. So, if he does that for me, I say thank you so much, and really enjoy this favor. Do you get what I mean?
- Celebrate Mondays or the full moon. Throw a party at home, just because parties are fun!
- The list goes on and on. Please let me know what you write down here that brings more joy into your home!

Try new things. Try for a week or longer. Don't give up at the first attempt to create joy at home, if you've been having a difficult time recently. Just do it, and I promise you, things will change. And if you have the best relationships under your roof already, your home will thrive even more. That's what I love about all these little things: They make the world (your home) a better place, wherever your starting point is!

Now let's take it to the streets. Do you know the term, "a random act of kindness"? It's a creative playground to bring more fun, lightness, happiness, and good mood into your neighborhood, village, city, or country. And with social media, you can influence even more people by showing off what your idea is. So, people around the globe can steal that idea from you, and do it in their own neighborhood. This ripple effect makes me happy just by writing about it.

The most important thing is that YOU have fun doing these random acts of kindness. Do what suits you, okay? If you have a smile on your face while preparing the action, you win twice over—or even more.

I have loads of ideas, little, and big ones. Not all of them will be possible to do, where you live, but they shall inspire your own creativity and your kind of fun and kindness.

Buy a package of sidewalk chalk, and go write or draw cool stuff onto the street!

**"Are you crazy, Ronja Sakata?
This makes me look super silly and childish!"**

Do you really care that much about what other people think of you? Screw them. You are bringing fun to the streets.
"No, I can't draw, and I won't write anything."
Hey, no problem! Just do what you LIKE to do.

Do it if you are an artistic person, or you just like the thought of writing a compliment, a wish, or even an inspirational quote on the ground like, "You are beautiful, inside and out!", "I wish you a wonderful day!", "You rock!", "Go for it!", "Don't let fear stand in the way of your dreams!", or "Nothing is impossible!". I think you get what I mean... Just play around, like a kid!

Draw a hopscotch on the sidewalk, and place a stone there so that everyone passing by can hop for fun. There are videos on Facebook with hidden cameras, where random people, grownups of all age groups, hop through with a big smile. Maybe you can install a hidden camera, too? Or hide with a camera behind the bushes? No, if that's too weird, don't do it! Just enjoy that you brought happiness into these people's lives with an effort of three minutes and some chalk. That's so worth it, right?

What's very cool and easy with sidewalk chalk, too, is a treasure hunt. With arrows and signs and maybe little letters, you can create a whole circuit for anybody who is in for some fun. This can be a really big thing in your neighborhood. Imagine how everybody would want to go on your treasure-hunt circuit-tour—and the video of it will go viral, and Ellen would invite you to her show. How about that?

You don't want ALL that? No problem. Just don't share it on social media. But please, if you do something cool, just because of this book, and I inspired you, and you're proud of it, would you be so kind as to send me a pic or a video? hello@ronjasakata.com. Thank you!

Up until now, it was a chalk-game. What about little notes? I had this idea of the Joy-Ripple-Effect a year ago and created the joy-cards, where you have templates with nice messages or plain ones for your own messages. On the next two pages, you'll see joy-cards for you to cut out of the book or to copy. Stick them everywhere you go—in public transportation, underneath a windshield wiper, in a shopping cart, on a can of pineapples... put the joy cards wherever you want, and let your message bring out a smile on the finder's face! The link on the card, www.joyismycompass.com/jre, leads to a free Joy Challenge with lots of little inspirations on how we can pass them on and put momentum on the Joy-Ripple-Effect.

I know, I know, I overuse the word JOY. But I deeply believe that we need more joy on our planet, and it starts with YOU, ourselves, and then our homes, and then our neighborhoods, and then our cities, and then our countries... I literally see the waves of the ripples flowing outwards, like on a lake. This is a real thing. You being kind to YOURSELF first, to others second, and they pass it on, and so on. YOU have an insanely huge impact on the planet. Yes, you alone. The power of one kind word, the magic of one random act of kindness... thank you for changing the world. Thank you!

Cut out the following page and tape the cards to lamp posts and park benches in your neighbourhood! If you don't want to ruin this book or the page is missing already, you'll find the templates on the book page:

www.joyismycompass.com/bookbonus

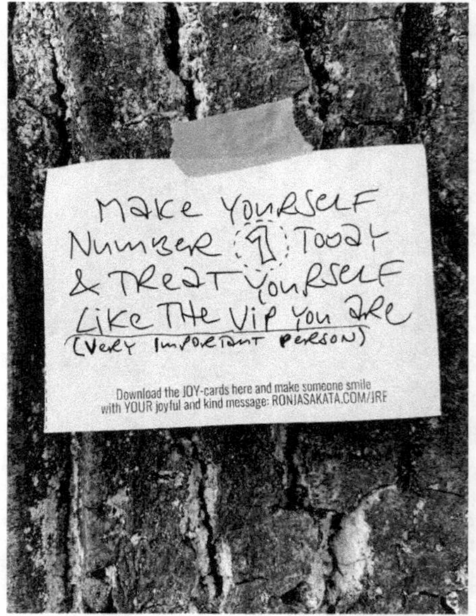

HEY SUPERSTAR, HOW
ARE YOU? I WISH
YOU A WONDERFUL
BEAUTIFUL DAY! ♡

YOU ARE POWERFUL,
YOU ARE BEAUTIFUL,
YOU ARE MAGICAL,
YOU ARE _YOU_ enjoy
one of a kind   Being
                       you!

YOU ARE THE MOST
IMPORTANT PERSON
IN YOUR LIFE! YOU
ARE WITH YOU 24/7! ☆
HOW ABOUT BECOMING
YOUR VERY BEST FRIEND?

YOU ARE ENOUGH!
NO, YOU ARE MORE
THAN ENOUGH!
YOU ARE _WONDERFUL!_

DO YOU KNOW WHAT
BRINGS YOU JOY?
HOW ABOUT DOING AT
LEAST 3 THINGS TODAY,
WHICH BRING YOU JOY?
↳ using your favorite coffee-mug
↳ dancing through your livingroom ....

SENDING YOU LOVE &
GOOD VIBES! HAVE A
WONDERFUL DAY FULL
OF BEAUTIFUL MOMENTS!

MAKE YOURSELF
NUMBER (1) TODAY
& TREAT YOURSELF
        YOURSELF
LIKE THE VIP YOU ARE
(VERY IMPORTANT PERSON)

WHAT IS YOUR FAVORITE
MEAL? HOW ABOUT
COOKING THIS DISH
TODAY JUST FOR YOU?

Write your own messages on the next page!
Or download the template on the book-bonus page:

www.joyismycompass.com/bookbonus

You go girl! And thank you for spreading kind messages!

Download the JOY-cards here and make someone smile
ith YOUR joyful and kind message: RONJASAKATA.COM/JRE

Download the JOY-cards here and make someone smile
with YOUR joyful and kind message: RONJASAKATA.COM/JRE

Download the JOY-cards here and make someone smile
ith YOUR joyful and kind message: RONJASAKATA.COM/JRE

Download the JOY-cards here and make someone smile
with YOUR joyful and kind message: RONJASAKATA.COM/JRE

Download the JOY-cards here and make someone smile
ith YOUR joyful and kind message: RONJASAKATA.COM/JRE

Download the JOY-cards here and make someone smile
with YOUR joyful and kind message: RONJASAKATA.COM/JRE

Download the JOY-cards here and make someone smile
ith YOUR joyful and kind message: RONJASAKATA.COM/JRE

Download the JOY-cards here and make someone smile
with YOUR joyful and kind message: RONJASAKATA.COM/JRE

If you are in for putting some money in the game, that's great fun too! A message (joy card or not) that says: "Hey my friend, this is for you, buy something nice", and you attach one or five or ten or twenty or fifty dollars to the note... wow, imagine the expression on the person's face who finds this blessing. "Where shall I put this?" Wrap it around a tree, on a park bench... wherever!

But it doesn't always have to be a surprising act of kindness. Just starting a genuine conversation with a homeless person, asking about his or her day can be a blessing too. Listening and being present. That's a big thing in today's world—not only with a homeless person, but with anybody you meet.

What's also very cool is to give compliments often. To complete strangers! It's so very interesting how they'll be received. A compliment? From a lady I don't know? What is her intention? If you just walk ahead, she or he may be stuck in their tracks for a moment, but after that, for sure, they will smile and take it all in! A compliment is like a huge gift! Only give a compliment if you really feel that way. Fake compliments stink! Think about how you receive compliments? Do you say: "Thank you very much!" or "That's so kind, thank you!" or do you dismiss it with an immediate compliment back, or play it down? This is SO interesting! It depends a lot on how you learned this as a kid. Being confident and proud of ourselves is something we can relearn if it was a no-go as a kid. Give compliments often, and try to receive them with a simple, "thank you." That's so good!

And the last thing: Have fun, wherever, whenever possible. If there is a slide, go slide down. If there is a swing, go swing. If you can bring fun into a meeting, a dinner gathering, a personal conversation, create joy for yourself and the others. Remember the one-hundred-things-that-bring-you-joy list? This list is GOLDEN, and you can write more things on the list every day. This list is the library of creating joy for yourself and the people around you in all the seasons and in all situations.

How about having a nice chat with your future self again? What is she doing to create joy all day long? She's freaking good at this joy game. She's so popular in her job, at home, in her neighborhood. Not in the "showing off" sense of popular—she just makes everybody feel so good when they spend time with her. She sees people. She's present. She listens. She is such a kind lady, a really genuine woman who is so inspiring to everyone around her. She chose herself. Everybody can tell that. She's just *herself.* She doesn't give a fuck about what the people around her say or think about her. She's doing her thing, and that is, to enjoy this fabulous life. To create every day as ideally as she can. She grows with her habits. She's taking care of her body and her soul. She's confident. She's not conceited at all. She has her fears and doubts, but she walks through them with the trusting feeling that she'll be okay. She is such a great woman, living her life without regrets, making memories with the people she loves, bringing fun and joy to everyone who spends time with her.

She is you! You just have a journey in front of you to become this lady! Or a different fabulous one. YOU choose! You have complete power over this transformation, and only you know how far away you are from this annoying superwoman who has all her shit together! Don't be jealous. Enjoy the journey to becoming her.

You don't go to the movies to only watch the happy ending. You want to see the whole movie. You don't go to a concert only to listen to the last song. You want to listen to the whole concert. Enjoy your journey. But always be aware that not one day is guaranteed. For me, it's a mix between self-care and pushing myself forward, a balance between chasing my goals and just enjoying the moment and chilling out. This is the art of living life in and out of our comfort zones, but holding our own standards high and focusing on creating JOY.

Your compass is now set. You are good to go do this. Every day, go out there and ROCK your life. Change takes time, but go all-in. I'm so proud of you that you read this book. Thank you for spending time with me! Thank you for being YOU! I love you right now, and I'm secretly even more in love with your future self! I'm cheering you on, and if our paths ever cross, I'll congratulate you personally for creating your glorious life, day by day! Take good care of yourself, and use this JOY-compass every day.

THESE
MAGICAL BUBBLES
MAKE YOUR WISHES
COME TRUE!

YOUR BOOK
BONUS
DOWNLOAD
LINK FOR
EVEN MORE
MAGIC

www.joyismycompass.com/bookbonus

CAN YOU HELP?

Thank you for reading my book!

I really appreciate all of your feedback, and I love hearing what you have to say. I need your input to make the next version of this book and my future books better.

Please leave me an honest review on Amazon letting me know what you thought of the book.

Thanks so much!

Ronja ♡

People That Have Inspired Me

- Brendon Burchard
  He wrote so many books, and you have to read them all! ;)
  High Performance Habits and *Life's Golden Ticket* are my
  most favorite for sure! Thanks to Brendon's live event
  Experts Academy I met the most amazing people, and I got
  to see Bo Eason live.

- Bo Eason
  I love Bo Eason, the author of *There Is No Plan B for Your
  A-Game*! He's a former football pro, who played in the
  Superbowl, before he smashed his knee for the 7th time
  ending his career. Check out what he did next. He's on
  YouTube with his mind blowing story telling power. I'll put
  the links to my favorite videos of Bo on the book-bonus
  page, ok? I met Bo in California at his live event, and I can
  highly recommend getting near this powerhouse. His
  energy is contagious and his expertise just brilliant.

- Jesse Itzler
  Living with a SEAL and *Living with the Monks* – these two
  books, you must listen to. Jesse is the guy, who invented
  "The Happiness Meter", and I told you about his Ted Talk
  in my book. I'm in one of Jesse's programs called BYLR
  (Build Your Life Resume), and I again met the coolest and
  most wonderful guys and girls.

- Sara Blakley

  She became the world's youngest female self-made billionaire in 2012. Jesse Itzler is her husband, and I admire how these two totally different, super inspiring people create their life together full of adventure, fun, and with a free spirit! Follow both of them on social media and get inspired!

- Leonie Dawson

  She taught me about not settling down in Stuckville, just travel through! Best analogy ever for being an entrepreneur.

- Adriene Michler

  This lady is my personal trainer in my living room at 4:44 or later in the day. If you want to try Yoga in secret, this is my recommendation: Yoga with Adriene. But there are loads of guys out there too. Check them out, yoga is cool!

References

These books had a big impact on my mindset and how I do life, so I can highly recommend them to you!

- Bronnie Ware, *The Top Five Regrets of the Dying*, Hay House Inc., 2019
  I started the book with these, do you remember? The book is very eye opening to all the things we could do NOW, when we're here and not when we're about to die.

- James Clear, *Atomic Habits*, Avery, 2018
  This is a MUST read. Really. Mandatory. No joke. Read this book next.

- Jens Corssen, *The Way of the Self-Developer*, Pronoun, 2016
  This book honestly changed my life. I listened to it on repeat, and I could tell you all of his stories and insights for eight hours straight. Read it too!

- Marie Kondo, *Magic Cleaning*, Ten Speed Press, 2014
  If you read this book or watch videos of her work online, your decluttering game will get stronger for sure!

- "self-care / self-'ker / noun", Lexico.com, 2021, https://www.lexico.com (11 March 2021)

About Me

You know a lot about me after reading this book already. I grew up on a construction site in a tiny village in the countryside of Switzerland and I loved it. My parents renovated a giant old house with their friends while raising my sister and me. I earned my first pocket money by knocking off old plaster work from walls. My dream job? Primary school teacher. When it was actually time to choose, I wanted to know more about the human body, about chemistry, about mechanics and process engineering. I loved watching Sesame Street, especially when they showed how something is made. I've always loved food and so: Food engineer, that was it! Studying this was the best decision, mostly because I met my best friends for life, and the student parties were so much fun!

I was a very insecure and shy kid when I was young. In school, I often got bullied. It wasn't until I was twenty years old and studying at the ETH Zürich that I finally felt for the first time: „This is good!" Finally I wasn't trapped in a classroom with a random bunch of kids. I was free to choose which of these 300 people in an auditorium I wanted to spend time with. Because of my studies I had to do a four-month long internship somewhere on this planet. That was destiny calling for real.

I found a company in Japan that was willing to let this Swiss girl work there, and they were even producing all the cool food:

Chewing gum, ice cream, chocolate, candy, instant noodle soups, and instant drinks. I hated languages at school, but there I learned Japanese like a champ. And one day, underneath the blooming cherry trees at the Hanami BBQ, I met my man. He was working at the chewing gum factory making three tons of fruit gum every single day. We had hoped for an endless summer in Japan, but I had to go home and finish my studies. Two times we said goodbye at the airport and it broke our hearts. We decided that we can't do this anymore and got married. Ken's first job after moving to Switzerland was at a sushi bar. His Japanese boss, hired me right after university to build a Japanese salad dressing company for him. I started in a backyard-production-room which was so filthy that I had to clean it for weeks before I could even start. When I landed the first article in a major Swiss newspaper with pics of me and my whole love story, things got busy. I made the sauce in forty liter containers, then filled the bottles and even labeled them by hand, at first. People were waiting next to the fridge in the fancy supermarket when I arrived sweaty on my bicycle with the next three boxes of salad dressing. Only a month earlier, they put three bottles of each flavor onto the shelf, and the store manager moaned: "They'll still be here by Christmas." Well, in August we sold 600 bottles in one week. Thank you, dear journalist for that article and thank you my sister and boyfriend, who came and helped me with the production working 20 hours per day. After three years, three friends and I took over the company and today my salad dressing baby is a full-grown production with many more products, thanks to my co-owner who is now the boss over there. I then started my Japan-information business while working as a teacher for food technologists and also still working at the salad dressing production. If you speak Swiss German you can even learn Japanese with my first online course I ever produced. But over the years I've come to realize my true calling: I want to inspire the whole wide world to find out "What do I want?" and help people focus on JOY! Today I'm super happy with my Joy business where I can help you in my 1:1 coaching, my Joy Mastermind (group coaching), and my Joy Academy (self-study course) to create your dream life and the best habits to reach all your goals on every single spoke of the wheel of life. In my newest addition, the Joy Podcast, I interview people like YOU and listen to stories of your life on how you create joy for yourself and others, and also about your struggles and how you overcame them. You are the expert of your own life and your story matters to the world! This book was the missing puzzle piece for reaching YOU. Mission accomplished. Thank you so much for being here! If you want to connect with me, check the next page where I list all the ways we can talk and work together.

Next Steps to Working With Me

Joy Academy

Check out my yearlong self-study coaching program, where you can change your life from whatever starting point into your dreamlife, because you decide! Your mindset shifts into the direction YOU want. You take full responsibility for your thoughts, feelings, words, and your action.
www.joyismycompass.com/joyacademy

Joy Challenge

The email challenge with daily prompts to bring more joy into your life and the ones around you. This is also the place where the JOY-cards lead to. Try it out and tell all your friends about it. I get such great responses about how this challenge changes things for the better! Once again, it's because you take time for yourself! You are the most important person in your life!
www.joyismycompass.com/jre

UA-Webinar

Do you want to hire a Universal assistant who helps you with all the invisible stuff and the things you can't control? Sign up here for my fun, free webinar and find out what a cool tool this is:
www.joyismycompass.com/ua

Private Coaching

Get in touch and we'll find out, if I'm the right coach for you! If yes, brilliant. If not, I have a huge list of wonderful coaches I can recommend to you!
www.joyismycompass.com/site/contact

Social Media

Let's get in touch on all the social media channels and on the book-bonus page. If you share your book experience on your channels and tag me, I'll gladly repost it. You can find me across all Social Media channels @joyismycompass and @ronjasakata.

Thank You!

Thank you for making this book possible, my gang of dear people near and far!

Thank you, Silvia! You let me share my version of your story, when we stood at Patrick's open grave in 1994 and the world changed forever. We've known each other since we were babies, but our deep friendship started back then when we were grieving together. Being forced to look a sudden death in the eyes and find out what that means about LIFE, changed me in my core. Thank you for being together with me on this road into the future in good and bad times!

My biggest thank you goes to my world's best assistant, Fiona. You not only formatted the whole book, but you also coached me through the whole year 2020, when I began my writing journey, and you pushed me in your loving way over the finish line. If you want to achieve great goals, hire a Fiona and celebrate her every day! I sure do! Thank you so much for your ongoing support and your insightful way of cheering me on, I couldn't have done it without you!

Thank you so, so much for editing my lousy English to an actual book, dear Lucretia! Your professionality and your close attention to details made this book possible. Thank you for understanding my "Swiss German-English". Luckily you speak both languages perfectly and knew what I wanted to say, even though I didn't get it right the first time. We have been friends for over 25 years, and it's such a great feeling to have accomplished this book together with you! Thank you for everything!!

Thank you, Qat, my second editor, for your great work. I got called out many times by you, and that made this book better, more streamlined and on point!

Thank you, Gary, my book coach from the wonderful program Self-Publishing School! The coaching call I remember best was during our ski vacation (I wrote every morning in the hotel room at 5am before my family woke up), and Ken said afterwards: “Gary sure says "amazing" a lot”. Thank you for cheering me on and teaching me your expertise!

Thank you, Greg, for your generosity and for making my longtime dream of writing a book become a reality: "Here is a course, use it well and get your book done!" I will be grateful for your gift forever, seriously!

Thank you my dear Bry for your magic! You took all the pictures of me for this book! Our photo shooting week that we spent together with your husband Alec and your two huskies in my grandfather's mountain cabin in the Swiss mountains is one of my favorite weeks ever. We had so much fun and the love and high vibes are ingrained into the pictures. So my dear reader, if you need pictures of yourself, that actually show your soul: Book Bry as fast as you can! You can find her here: brypenney.com

A big thank you goes to my family: Thank you, my dear parents, you taught me that I could do whatever I want. I just have to find out how and then do it. Thank you, Ken, my man, for everything! Our journey of twenty years and counting is simply wonderful! You have taught me countless lessons in our marriage about independence, communicating right in the moment, and supporting each other's dreams. Thank you for our life! Thank you, Mika, for being our daughter, bringing the world of tomorrow into our home with all your ideas, your confidence, your free spirit. Thank you for being you, my love!

Thank YOU, my dear reader, for buying and reading this book! It's my honor and pleasure to cheer you on and hold the space for your dreams and your big vision. Let's create so much JOY in our lives, and let's change the world together, ok? If you want to meet me: Join the Joy Academy or follow me on all the social media channels. Thank you for your honest book review and your feedback. I'll repost your posts with a big grateful smile if you tell your friends about this book. Thank you for being YOU! The world needs your power, your talents, and your JOY.

Lots of love,

Ronja